COMMUNITY CARE FOR MENTALLY HANDICAPPED CHILDREN

CONTEMPORARY ISSUES IN SOCIAL SCIENCES

This is series addresses current debates in the Social Sciences.
Short books will be authored by experienced academics with active
research interests in the relevant areas. Collections of papers
reporting up-to-date research on a single issue or theme will also
form part of the series, as well literature reviews and evaluations of
public policy.

Current Titles

Pamela Abbott & Roger Sapsford :   Community Care for Mentally

Handicapped Children

Allan Cochrane :   Developing Local Economic Strategies

Doreen Massey :   Nicaragua

COMMUNITY CARE FOR MENTALLY HANDICAPPED CHILDREN

PAMELA ABBOTT
ROGER SAPSFORD

Open University Press
Milton Keynes — Philadelphia

Open University Press
Open University Educational Enterprises Limited
12 Cotteridge Close
Stony Stratford
Milton Keynes   MK11 1BY, England

and

242 Cherry Street
Philadelphia, PA 19106, USA

First Published 1987

British Library Cataloguing in Publication Data
Abbot, Pamela
    Community care for mentally handicapped children
    (Contemporary issues in social sciences series).
1. Mentally handicapped children – Care and treatment – Great Britain
I. Title II. Sapsford, R.J. III. Series
362.3'58'088054   HV901.G7
ISBN 0-335-15523-5   (pbk)
Library of Congress Cataloging-in-Publication Data
Abbott, Pamela.
    Community care for mentally handicapped children.
    Bibliography: p.
    1. Mentally handicapped children – Services for – Great Britain –
    History.
    2. Mentally handicapped children – Government policy – Great
    Britain – History.
    3. Mentally handicapped children – Great Britain – Family
    relationships. I. Sapsford, Roger II. Title
HV901. G7A33 1987   362.3'088054   87-22040
ISBN 0-335-15523-5   (pbk)
Printed in Great Britain by J. W. Arrowsmith Ltd, Bristol.

CONTENTS

INTRODUCTION

Mental handicap is not a 'thing' but to a large extent a 'construction'; its nature varies from time to time and from place to place. The real nature of stupidity in any given society is a matter of labelling. All societies have some people who are less intelligent or less competent than others, but in most they are not specially picked out as a deviant class or group in need or special treatment or management; indeed, in some they are not even at any particular disadvantage. In others, however, there is a labelled group of 'retarded' or 'handicapped' people who are managed in particular ways – largely to their disadvantage. We accept Blumer's dictum that:

> Social problems are not the result of an intrinsic malfunctioning of society, but are a result of a process of definition in which a given condition is picked out and identified as a social problem.
> (Blumer,1971, p 301)

In the first of these two papers we look at the origins of mental handicap as a 'social problem' in England and the United States. We argue that the process by which mental handicap came to be defined in

1

the West as a distinct condition and as a social problem can be seen as an outcome of the concurrent development of industrial capitalism. In a society which was dependent on the orderly exploitation of abstracted labour, those who could not or would not participate in the labour process quickly became targets for an 'attitude' of fear and distrust which can readily be seen as expressing underlying particula interests. The simultaneous development of the institution of compulsory schooling – itself susceptible to similar analysis – rendered the mentally handicapped visible and thereby made them a specific target for labelling. Institutions were developed for the treatment, or rather the handling, of the 'problem': the retarded were segregated and prevented from breeding, partly 'for their own protection', but predominantly for society's.

During this century the place of mental handicap in the dominant ideology has changed markedly, and with it the institutions of 'treatment'. Mental handicap is no longer feared as a 'social problem' in the way that the nineteenth century feared it; the retarded are no longer seen as a threat to society, but rather as just another 'problem group' for whom social provision has to be made. Simultaneously the dominant form of 'treatment' has changed from segregation and incarceration to the cheaper alternative of 'community care' – cheaper, that is, because the change has been accompanied by a massive withdrawal of resources. The result is undoubtedly a better life for mentally handicapped people, and especially for mentally handicapped children. There is no evidence, however, that caring about their condition of life has ever been a factor influencing how mentally handicapped people are treated. Individuals may care passionately about their life-chances and work tirelessly in their cause, but the origins of the dominant mode of treatment in a given period can clearly be traced to structural socio-economic factors.

A critical analysis does not stop at this kind of structural determinism, however, but goes on to trace the impact of structures on people's lives, the experiential correlates of social structure and the constraints (and self-constraints) imposed on autonomy of action. The second paper in this volume, therefore, goes on to look at the 'community care' of mentally handicapped children as it is currently practised, in part through the eyes of those on whom the care predominantly falls – namely, the mothers. The views and experiences

2

of mothers with mentally handicapped children are contrasted with those of mothers whose children do not bear this label, to illustrate the general constraints child-care imposes on women and to distinguish the specific extra burden which falls on women with mentally handicapped children. We look at how this 'problem class' (the mothers) cope with their burden, what help they receive, how they construe and manage their lives and what they forsee as their future. We hope thereby to illustrate the consequences of a social policy at a personal level and to illustrate the 'double bind' of conflicting real interests to which mothers may be exposed. The link between the two papers is that the current lives of mothers, described in the second, are in part determined by and an expression of the historical developmental described in the first. They are of course directly affected by historical developments in policies concerning the 'treatment' or 'handling' of their children, but there are also links which are less palpable, though no less real. Current stereotypes of mental handicap, for instance, can be traced directly to the Eugenics campaigns in the early years of the century. The way that mothers of mentally handicapped children take their 'responsibilities for granted, however, expresses the same history in less obvious form; the current discourse expresses history, and history helps us to understand its implications.

By 'mental handicap' in these papers we generally mean the full range of disabilities popularly comprehended under that label. The mothers we interviewed for the second paper had children with very diverse degrees of mental and physical handicap; in the first paper, following the concerns of the times, most of the discussion centres around 'mild' handicap, but we remain alert to the fate of others. We follow the general English terminology in distinguishing 'severe' handicap - those with measured IQ of 50 or less, whose condition is generally traceable either to gross physical damage or to a genetic and sometimes a hereditable condition such as phenylketonuria or Down's Syndrome - from 'mild' handicap, with measured IQs of 50-70 and far less readily traceable to physical origins. (The position of Down's Syndrome children is ambivalent; they are generally classified en masse as severely retarded, perhaps because of the obvious physical origin of their condition, but their measured IQs may often be in excess of 50. Sometimes, therefore, we have considered them separately in the analysis.) We are aware of and have discussed elsewhere (Abbott and

3

Sapsford, 1986) the extraordinary variety of lives and conditions which the label 'mental handicap' comprehends. The inclusion of such a variety of different and unrelated conditions under the one label itself demonstrates the degree to which the concept is a social construct, designed for an administrative purpose.

In concentrating on the social and personal construction of mental handicap — the implications of the label as negotiated between individuals, construed through ideological categories and sustained through social institutions — we do not mean to deny the 'reality' of the condition. 'Severe' mental handicap clearly covers a range of conditions of physical origin which involve real impairment of social and intellectual ability. We are less convinced that 'mild' handicap is anything more than a statistical artefact — in any normal distribution somebody has to lie on the left of the distribution — but we do not rule out the possibility of physical origins. Our point, however, is that almost everything that goes to make up the societal and familial reality of mental handicap is independent of the origins of the condition. 'Mental handicap' is defined and substantiated not by the condition of the individual, but by the actions of parents, the reactions of others around them, the wider ideology within which the concept is located, and the socially and historically determined institutions and resources which condition the lives of the individuals and those who care for them.

1 INDUSTRIALISATION AND MENTAL HANDICAP: THE GROWTH OF A SOCIAL PROBLEM

Introduction

One of the main problems in developing a historical perspective on mental handicap is precisely that there is little evidence on attitudes specifically towards the mentally handicapped and the handling of them before the nineteenth century. It seems inconceivable to the modern mind, but mentally handicapped people do not seem to have been recognised as a social problem – or indeed as a distinct group of people – until the eighteenth century. There is litle or no discussion in Mediaeval literature of what we would now call 'mild mental handicap' and little reflection of its existence as a distinct problem in Mediaeval practice. Even severe handicap receives little mention in the medical literature, though non-medical literature mentions endemic goitre and cretinism, and cretins are depicted as fools or monsters in paintings of the thirteenth and fourteenth centuries. English law first came to make some distinction between persons temporarily non compos mentis and 'natural fools' in the reign of Edward II, with regard to the protection of property (which in the case of the latter passed into the king's stewardship). However the tests used readily confused the two classes and only those individuals who owned land would have come within the purview of the law – probably a very small minority of the mentally disordered.

There is no evidence that the majority of those whom society now labels 'mentally handicapped' were labelled as deviant in the early Middle Ages; indeed all the evidence points the other way. Most of those who are now labelled as mildly or even moderately handicapped would have been perfectly competent to work the land – perhaps under family guidance – and to carry out the rest of the daily tasks required of them. For those who <u>were</u> labelled as deviant, treatment varied very widely. The mentally handicapped who were unable to fill a more stable niche in the social order were in the same case as other dependent persons – cared for by the monasteries or by their families, or most probably left to wander as beggars and seek Christian charity. With the gradual breakdown of the feudal economic order from the fourteenth century and the increase in the number of beggars and vagrants, attitudes began to harden against the dispossessed and the dependent. Laws were promulgated that able-bodied beggars should not be given aid, and restricting the movement of serfs and the indigent poor. This brought about a change in the philosophy underlying charity. The impotent poor (the old, the sick and the obviously handicapped) were entitled to assistance out of public funds or from charities. The able-bodied (a group that would have included the 'incompetent' as well as the idle) were not. One should note, however, that a majority of those now labelled as mildly handicapped would <u>not</u> have been seen as totally socially incompetent in a predominantly agricultural and home-based system of production; they would have found, or been found, a productive role.

This paper traces the history of mental handicap's gradual emergence and problematisation, from the Reformation and the Englightenment through the development and elaboration of industrial capitalism in England and America and into the twentieth century. We find that mental handicap 'progresses' during this period from not being recognised at all as a distinctive 'class' and an object of policy, through belief in curability, to fear of 'the mob' which becomes progressively specialised as fear that those who cannot or will not work will undermine the economic base of society and then that the workforce itself was showing dangerous signs of degeneration. We trace the concurrent 'progress' in treatment, from institutionalisation for purposes of treatment to institutionalised segregation and possibly even sterilisation for public protection, and out again into the state advocacy of a policy of 'community care'.

An examination of historical attitudes towards and social provision made for deviant groups, with special reference to the mentally subnormal, should enable us to understand the relationships between socioeconomic structures, socially constructed attitudes towards the subnormal and the type of provision made for those labelled and managed as deviants. While it is clear that there is a relationship between social perceptions of deviants and the way they are controlled, what is less obvious is why the mentally handicapped are cast in different roles in different societies or at different times. What we intend in this paper is to illustrate how the way a society 'sees' its deviants is inextricably linked to its norms and values, themselves a reflection of the dominant ideology. (This is not to suggest a Zeitgeist, a single and coherent attitude corresponding to a given period, but that there is a clear relationship between prevailing social structures, dominant ideology and the way society handles its deviants.)

The Reformation and the Enlightenment
Indigence or care at home
If the Mediaeval system of handling deviants may be seen as one based on the community and the family, the period from the sixteenth to the eighteenth century marks a gradual transition to a system based on institutions and administered by central government. Political factors — the struggle of the Crown to augment state power at the expense of the church — combined with economic factors and a change in the basic form of religious ideology to bring about a fundamental change in how the mentally handicapped were viewed and how deviants in general were handled.

In the Middle Ages the Christian church had advocated charity towards those unable to care for themselves - love, understanding and respect as well as physical care. While such advocacy has never died out within the church, another view began to surface in the sixteenth century. For instance, Calvin and Luther both denounced the mentally

7

subnormal as possessed by Satan and without soul, fit only for destruction. While in Catholicism the road to salvation had been the 'communal' one of faithful membership in the Church, Protestantism began to advocate the 'individualist' view that the individual's own faith and conduct determined salvation and damnation. God and the devil came increasingly to be seen as at war for each individual soul, and the devil was to be resisted by whatever means seemed most appropriate. During this period the witch-hunts grew in importance and prevalence, and it has commonly been argued that the mentally ill and handicapped were prominent as victims of this form of 'popular justice'.

The witch-hunts may be overrated, however, as a total indicator of how a period and a system came to terms with the mentally abnormal. As Neugebauer points out as a result of studying legal provision,

> ... in the histories of ... psychiatry, macabre scenes of witch-hunts and witch burnings have commanded great fascination The existence and activities of an institution like the Court of Wards have been neglected ... But the picture of treatment ideals which emerges from this collection of legal documents is radically different from that which arises from those other judicial records, witch trials. Government involvement with Court of Wards cases was designated to protect the disturbed person and his property.
>
> (Neugebuer, 1978, p.167)

and

> In the Mediaeval period royal protection was linked with profit. In the sixteenth and seventeenth centuries this financial dimension gradually disappeared while the welfare aspect was significantly expanded.
>
> (p. 197)

He points out that while in the Mediaeval period the royal jurisdiction over the mentally disordered had been handled on an ad hoc and relatively informal basis, in 1540 an Act of Parliament brought them within the jurisdiction of the Courts of Wards and Liveries (abolished during the Civil War in the 1640s) and Guardians were required to care for the idiot and his family as well as manage his possessions. While in theory all mentally disordered subjects came within the province of

8

the Court and any person, with or without property, could be brought to official notice, in practice, since official referral depended mainly on private citizens (who hoped subsequently to obtain grants of control), only persons with wealth sufficient to bear the cost of court procedure were reported. Neugebauer, however, argues that an examination of cases handled by royal jurisdiction in the seventeenth century (the first reliable statistics) shows a fairly wide social class distribution. Forty per cent were from the landed gentry, twenty per cent women who were heiresses or widows, but the rest were tradesmen, yeomen or even agricultural workers.

The mentally subnormal did, however, continue to be regarded as figures of fun and to provide entertainment for the wealthy. Foucault (1971) has pointed out that the Bethlehem Asylum in London and the Bicetre Hospital in Paris were opened to visitors so that they could be entertained at the expense of the foolish and mad inmates. The Pennsylvanian Hospital (the first in the United State, opened in 1756) also put residents on display but at the expense of visitors; the hospital charged visitors a fee.

By the seventeenth century informed knowledge of the mentally handicapped was growing. Thomas Willis (1672) provides one of the earliest systematic discussions of mental subnormality. He distinguished clearly between mental handicap and mental illness. The mentally ill are 'foolish' while the mentally subnormal are 'stupid'. The mentally subnormal have a number of characteristics that can be used to identify them – they are defective in apprehension, memory and judgement, behave in a dull fashion and display stupidity in their expression. Willis suggests that mental deficiency is usually inherited, and the list of 'genetic causes' heralds those found in late nineteenth and early twentieth century accounts of subnormality and includes alcoholism, epilepsy and licentiousness among other degeneracies. He concludes that mental deficiency can be measured in terms of social adaptability, and though it is incurable some of the deficient can be helped to improve. John Locke (1690) also distinguished between mental subnormality and mental illness; however, like Willis', his classification seems to have more applicability to the middle and upper classes than to the majority of the population in seventeenth century England. Some years after the publication of

Locke's work Daniel Defoe (1697) advocated the provision of separate asylums for the mentally defective.

Despite gradually changing attitudes towards the mentally handicapped, the general, everyday social perception of subnormals changed little. They continued to be cared for by their families, or turned out to wander as beggars. Their 'treatment' tended therefore to be that afforded to the whole class of vagrants – a class which was beginning to be seen as a problem. During the sixteenth century the numbers of unemployed labourers increased as the enclosure movement continued, at the same time as the one major source of charity, the monasteries, had been dissolved and the Reformation had resulted in changed attitudes to the giving of alms. The large increase in the number of vagrants and beggars in England was seen as presenting a threat to law and order, the maintenance of which was essential to the construction of effective central government; consequently official policies to deal with poverty and the socially marginal groups were determined by the need to maintain law and order, which necessitated the suppression of vagancy and begging. As Foucault has pointed out:

> In the classical period indigence, laziness, vice and madness mingled in equal guilt with unreason. Mad men were caught in the great confinement of poverty and unemployment
> ...
> (Foucault, 1971, p.259)

Thus the English Poor Law Act (1601) focused attention on the poor and unemployed but made no separate provision for the mentally ill or handicapped. As a consequence harmless idiots and lunatics continued to be left at liberty as long as they were not considered to be dangerous and caused no social disturbance. If necessary, their relatives or others prepared to care for them were provided with a permanent pension for their support. Those who were seen as a danger to themselves or the community would probably have been chained in the few existing hospitals or in the Poor Law Institutes that started to be established from the 1630s. They may also have been chained in the 'houses of correction' whose construction an Act of 1575 had recommended.

The great confinement

By the end of the seventeenth century a change in social attitudes to marginal groups, including the mentally handicapped, was taking place; thus began the period of the 'Great Confinement', when idiots, lunatics, criminals, vagrants and the unemployed were seen as a 'threat' to society and were locked away. It is necessary to question what is meant, however, by 'threat' to society. We have argued that the increase in unemployment was a direct consequence of the process of enclosures and that a large number of idle people were seen as posing a direct threat to the established order and were consequently incarcerated. This does not fully explain why they were 'confined' rather than excluded in some other way from society, nor why those who were apparently harmless but without employment were also incarcerated. Foucault suggests that this was because it was idleness as such that was condemned, coming to be seen as 'the greatest sin' during the Reformation. Society could not allow people to remain idle because this would incur God's wrath. The obligation to work was an ethical exercise and a moral guarantee. Consequently the workhouse was not a mere refuge for the old, sick and infirm, nor just a forced labour camp, but also an institution responsible for correcting a certain moral 'abeyance'.

The first organised effort to provide for the mentally disordered in a total institution was in Paris at the Bicetre hospital established in the seventeenth century. In England the change was reflected in the increased use of Houses of Correction and the Workhouse to incarcerate deviants, and the development of the last of these was stimulated by an Act in 1714 that distinguished between the lunatics and rogues, vagabonds, sturdy beggars and vagrants. Two Justices of the Peace could order the confinement of the metally disordered, and one method that parishes adopted to 'deal' with them was to board them out in private houses, which gradually acquired the description of 'Mad' Houses. In the United States a system of 'boarding out' was also common – housing the mentally disabled with the bidder who asked the least fee for them – with obvious consequences.

During the eighteenth century, Houses of Correction and Poor Law Institutions acquired a new purpose in addition to that of providing for the unemployed in periods of crisis – that of regulating the economy. Thus a dual system of treatment of the mentally handicapped

11

developed in England.   Those with wealthy relatives, and some pauper lunatics, were sent to the private-enterprise mad houses, where they spent years chained up in terrible conditions.   Mad House owners were concerned with making profits, not with the care of their charges. Those whose relatives could not afford to pay the charges of the Mad House, along with the unemployed, the old and the sick, continued to be incarcerated in Poor Law Institutions, where the main emphasis was on putting them to work, making them economically productive (although this practice gradually fell into disuse as it was suggested that it took work away from 'honest' men in the community).

In everyday practice the mentally subnormal continued to be seen as an integral part of the marginal population - those unable to be economically productive and to take their place as full members of captalist society.   In legal terms, the distinction between mental subnormality and mental illness continued to be seen as important, because of the need to protect property rights.   The procedure was that a jury was used to determine whether a person was incapable of managing his own affairs, whether because of idiocy or lunacy, with mental ability judged by tests of practical competence: diagnosis was based on such inabilities as not being able to count to twenty, measure a yard of cloth, name the days of the week, answer questions concerned with his daily life, or learn to read.   In the eighteenth century British law continued to recognise, essentially, two categories - the idiot and the lunatic.   These were not medical categories but determined in relation to civil capacity and legal responsibility as judged by a jury.   Juries seldom found a man an idiot, but preferred to find him non compos mentis for a time.   In any case a man was only an idiot if he was judged totally devoid of intelligence.   The main legal concern was the protection of property; thus only those who owned or potentially controlled property would have been 'tested' to determine if they were incurably subnormal.   The vast majority of those incapable of supporting themselves financially would have been cared for by their families or incarcerated in Mad Houses or the Workhouse.

In the United States the early settlers found no cause to provide special treatment for mentally handicapped people.   Their social programme for dependent groups was based on the Elizabethan Poor Laws; responsibility for the poor rested with the local community, and mentally handicapped people were usually handled under the laws

12

developed for paupers, along with the sick, the insane and the elderly (see Deutsch, 1949). (The need for labour in the colonies did lead to one particularly American development, however (see Scherenberger, 1983) - the selling of the mildly handicapped into slavery or indenture.) Those who were not supported by their families nor able to work would either have finished up in jail as being a 'public nuisance' or been 'placed out' - boarded out with whoever was prepared to feed and house them at the lowest cost Although alms houses and work houses came to be opened from the late seventeenth century, they were not used extensively for mentally handicapped people until the growth of urban areas in the nineteenth century. The only institutions making provision for mentally handicapped people in the seventeenth and eighteenth centuries were a few hospitals - for example the Pennsylvanian Hospital (opened in 1756) and the Virginian Hospital (opened in 1773). The kind of 'treatment' and conditions provided resembled those found in hospitals and private mad houses in Britain (see Scherenberger, 1983).

Kathleen Jones has succinctly summed up the prevalent conception of mental disorder at the end of the eighteenth century in England:

> There was no clear distinction of what mental disorder was
> and certainly no recognition of the mentally ill or
> handicapped as a category requiring a distinct form of
> treatment. The problem was a submerged one ... If
> mental condition reduced them to penury they came within
> the purview of the Poor Law. If it led them to break the
> criminal code, they were judged by the penal law. If they
> wandered abroad from their legal place of settlement
> without means of support they were involved in the rigours
> of the vagrancy laws.
> (Jones, 1972, p 3)

With the qualifications of detail mentioned above, the situation was much the same in America. Mental disorder was explained in terms of supernatural forces, but the mentally handicapped were not seen as 'children of God' but as incarnations of the Devil or other evil spirits. The management of those of the mentally subnormal who were indeed managed along with other marginal group who were seen as a 'threat' to the developing socio-economic order was to incarcerate them, to protect society from the deviant. However, the majority

13

remained at liberty in the community, to be cared for by their families or to fend for themselves.

The Nineteenth Century: The Growth of Fear

During the nineteenth century a radical shift in practice came about. First the severely and then the mildly handicapped came to be seen as a distinct and serious 'problem class' in Britain and the United States (indeed, in the whole of the Western world), which called into action agents of social control. By the turn of the century biological theories relating to heredity and evolution, both reflecting and magnifying a growing fear of mental handicap as a 'social evil', came to play a dominant part in determining the ways in which society viewed the problem and the methods of handling it. (Indeed, some of the elements of these theories have passed into 'common ideology' and may still be observed underlying current popular attitudes.) A key point to note, however, is that these changes came about only as Britain and the United States move from a pre-industrial, pre-capitalist economic system towards industrial capitalism.

The size of the 'problem'

In the nineteenth century official and public reactions to the mentally handicapped, especially the 'feebleminded', were conditioned by the fact that they were seen as part of the 'dangerous classes' – a group that threatened the stability of society. This fear developed out of the fear of the mob that grew in late eighteenth century England with the beginnings of the modern working class. It was argued that there was a connection between poverty and moral degeneracy and hence with criminal behaviour; that is, the conditions of the poor became associated in the mind of the authorities with the preconditions of crime. This resulted in the production of a perceived deeper and more serious potential danger from the lower orders – a belief that poverty, bad habits and propensity to crime might provoke them into riotous behaviour and escalate into a threat to civil order itself. This led to a declension from the poor to the criminal classes to the 'dangerous classes'. With the example of the French Revolution still fresh in memory, the fear grew that the 'mob' or 'sunken ten per cent' would

14

contaminate the respectable working class and create social unrest. Victorian England's image of the poor as a dangerous residue resulted in them being regarded as an alien class, as human refuse, outside of civil society, a constant threat to the stability of society, a group that needed to be constrained and controlled, managed as deviants. Although by the end of the nineteenth century the fear was no longer the same of riots and rebellion, fear remained of the physical and mental degeneration of the race as the residuum bred faster than the respectable classes.

Political agitation at the end of the eighteenth century precipitated legal and political reform. It was clear that the older forms of social control could no longer withstand the industrial and economic change and the political challenge. Reform was the method by which the new social order was constructed, and in the process social control was strengthened and the threat of revolution held at bay (eg by changes in custodial institutions, including the workhouse, prisons and asylums). In the period up to 1850 Britain was transformed from a largely rural, basically agrarian economy to one which was urban, industrial and based on wage labour. State intervention increasingly attempted to segregate and classify the working class into various categories - the respectable and the non-respectable, the industrious and the dangerous. The latter group were conceptualised as a major threat to the social order and various ideological mechanisms, including charity and education, were utilised in an effort to moralise and regulate the behaviour, life-style and leisure activities of this group. (State policy continued to be heavily influenced by _laissez faire_ commitments, however, which continued to exert an influence on the form that social policy look well into the twentieth century. Policies had to be justified, both in terms of expenditure and by demonstrating a _need_ for state intervention.) This fear of the poor was not new in the nineteenth century but it took on a different dimension as social change heightened class consciousness and the problem took on a new level of intensity. Reforms were aimed at the maintenance of order; the evolutionary and benevolent conception of social reform is misleading. The attitude of reformers in the first part of the nineteenth century was that the idle needed to be disciplined, instilled with the habits of industry - but the need was for a particular type of disciplined individual to work in the factories.

Studies of the introduction of mass schooling in the nineteenth century suggest that it was seen as the solution to the problem of social control, in a situation where the family was no longer able 'adequately' to socialise children,

> Schools at once supply labour to the dominant enterprise and reinforce the racial, ethnic, sexual and class segregation of the labour force

and

> The emergence and evolution of this educational system ... (was an) ... outgrowth of the political and economic conflict arising from this continued widening and deepening of capitalist control over production ...
>
> (Bowles and Gintes, 1976, p.234)

While it can be argued that mass schooling became necessary because of technological changes or a demand for more 'educated' workers it was also clearly a measure aimed at social control, to check delinquency, encourage religious observance and inculcate a work discipline. (By the mid nineteenth century children were no longer employed in factories because of protective legislation and technological changes in the production process.)

The introduction of mass schooling resulted in the discovery of the 'feebleminded' children who appeared normal but who would not learn to conform to the educational system and consequently presented a problem. This group posed a 'threat' to the dominant ideology of the Protestant ethic - a group who could not support themselves economically and were dependent on society. These children came mainly from poor homes, frequently had unemployed, alcoholic, unmarried mothers and the mentally ill or other 'degenerates' for relatives. It was also observed that this group had larger families than average, and the fear grew that this group would swamp society and consequently posed a threat to civilisation. By the early twentieth century it was generally accepted that this group needed to be shut away and prevented from breeding for the protection of society.

Science, medicine and treatment

With the growth of capitalism and the challenge to religion by rational-scientific explanation there was a need to justify an unequal society, to develop an ideology that rationalised a particular kind of social relationship as natural, not on religious grounds but on scientific ones. Scientific theories replaced religion as the final arbiter of truth; that is, they were seen to provide value-free, reliable and valid accounts of the world. By the end of the nineteenth century scientific theories had been developed and purported to identify the mentally handicapped objectively and gave a scientific justification for policies of segregation or even sterilisation. However, theories develop in parallel with the particular circumstances of societies. Although the particular ways in which the mentally handicapped were viewed and treated reflects contemporary medical knowledge, they can be understood fully only in the context of Victorian attitudes to the marginal population.

Nonetheless the progress of knowledge in medicine is important for understanding developments in treatment ideology during the nineteenth century, which was when medical men fought for and won the right to adjudicate on what is to be seen as 'normal'. In the early part of the century it was thought possible, if not to cure idiocy, then at least to train idiots to become productive members of society. Condillac's 'associationism' – the view that sensation alone is the basis of mental life and that the environment determines human development – was put into practice by Itard in his treatment of an idiot named Victor, demonstrating, if not 'cure', at least improvement. Edouard Seguin, the first acknowledged teacher and leader in the specific field of mental handicap, was significantly influenced by Itard, and in turn popularised an 'environmental' approach through his textbook published in 1846 and widely read in Europe and in the United States. This was the period, in the early and mid nineteenth century, when professionals concerned with the mentally handicapped believed that the subnormal could be educated to a standard where they could play a full social and economic role in society. This view is well expressed in the first report of the trustees of one of the early schools for idiots in the United States:

> We do not propose to create or supply faculties absolutely
> wanting, nor to bring all grades of idiocy to the same

17

standard of development or discipline, nor to make them all capable of sustaining credibly all the relations of a social and mental life, but rather to give dormant faculties the greatest possible development and to apply these awakened faculties to a useful purpose under the control of an aroused and disciplined will. At the base of all our efforts the principle that, as a rule, none of the faculties are absolutely wanting ...

(Trustees of the State of New York School for Idiots, 1852)

Despite the optimistic view that mentally handicapped people could be trained or educated to take their place in production the majority continued to receive no special training or treatment. Schools for the mentally handicapped began to appear in England and America from about 1840. However, in Britain by 1881 only three per cent of identified idiots were in public institutions specifically designated for the subnormal (Charities Organisation Society, 1877); there were over thirteen thousand mentally handicapped people in American almshouses alone, as late as 1910 (US Department of Commerce, 1914). The majority continued to be handled with the rest of the 'marginal population'. Those who were able, worked; the remainder were supported by their families or warehoused in almshouses, work houses, jails or lunatic asylums.

Science, heredity and the protection of society

With the size of the 'problem' thus 'revealed', and the feasibility of education challenged, policy began to change. While special education was established for the mildly handicapped in both countries, at the same time large institutions were built which were designed to provide life-long care for all grades of handicap. The change was reinforced and given a particular direction by a change in 'scientific' views which suggested that segregation in institutions was not only expedient but also necessary for society's survival – the growing view that retardation was hereditary, passed on from generation to generation and associated with other forms of degeneracy. Attitudes towards the subnormal and especially the feebleminded began to change; they began to be regarded as a threat to racial survival and as a life-long burden on society – as presenting, in other words, a real and distinct social

18

problem. The idea began to circulate that there was a need to protect society from these 'dangerous' groups not only as part of the general fear that the dangerous classes would contaminate the respectable working classes but also because of the fear that by their propensity to breed the social degenerates would grow in numbers, posing a threat to civilisation. The major developments in social policy which followed from this view can be seen in the early twentieth century but their seeds are to be seen in the nineteenth.

One of the first experts to claim that mental deficiency was a hereditary trait was Howe (1848), who considered it a condition inflicted on those whose parents 'violated the natural laws of man' — ie paupers, alcoholics, petty criminals. According to Howe, not only was such degeneracy passed on from generation to generation, but

> Idiots form one rank of that fearful host which is ever
> pressing upon society with its suffering, miseries and its
> crimes and which society is ever trying to hold off at
> arm's length – to keep in quarantine, to shut up in jails
> and almshouses or at least to treat as a pariah caste.
> (p.1)

The fear of social degeneracy and the perceived need to protect society from them grew steadily in the second half of the nineteenth century. The main emphasis also changed, under the growing influence of Social Darwinism and its outgrowths in Degeneracy Theory and the Eugenics Movement, from training for production to warehousing for the protection of society.

Degeneracy Theory was first developed by a Frenchman, Morel, in the 1850s. Degeneracy Theory essentially held:

(1) that hereditary taint is polymorphous – that is, the degenerative tendency expresses itself in different ways and with different forms of deviance;

(2) that acquired traits are transmitted to, and thus that parental experiences have an effect on, the offspring;

and

(3) that the condition would become progressively worse from generation to generation if not checked.

(The second of these hypotheses was widely accepted in the nineteenth century, and its adherents included Darwin and Spencer. The first and third of them profoundly influenced the 'proofs' of heredity put

19

forward in the early twentieth century – see below.) However, while Morel and Howe accepted degeneration, they did not subscribe to the 'pessimistic' or 'alarmist' attitudes to the problem of mental handicap which began to develop in the late nineteenth century. The acceptance of a hereditarian view which allowed for the transmission of environmental effects would not in itself lead to pessimism – one could alter the environment and consquently forestall or reverse degeneration. (In fact, the pessimistic implication does not appear even to have occurred to Howe or Morel.)

It was the Darwinian Theory of Evolution, combined with the theory of degeneration, that contributed to a radically different perception of the mentally handicapped. The theory of evolution and the idea of the survival of the fittest in the struggle for existence put degeneration in a broader context: the physically and mentally unfit are no longer seen as the unfortunate victims of the environment and/or hereditary taint but as demonstrably members of an inferior race which ought to be allowed to die out as quickly as possible. (Note that no special theory of degeneration is needed for this purpose; many Social Darwinians systematically applied the theory of the survival of the fittest without reference to degeneration, simply maintaining that deviant members of society had proved themselves unfit.)

However, Social Darwinism, which so profoundly influenced the Eugenics Movement, was not simply the product of evolutionary theory. Its roots can be traced back to classical economic theory, especially Smith's advocacy of free competition in the market place and the Malthusian Theory of Population. Spencer, ten years before the 'Origin of Species' was published, expressed views about how society should deal with the incapable that find an echo in Social Darwinism:

> Blind to the fact that under the natural order of things society is constantly excreting its unhealthy, imbecile, slow, vacillating, faithless members, these unthinking, though well meaning, men advocate an interference which not only stops the purifying process but even increases the vitiation – absolutely encourages the multiplication of the reckless and incompetent by offering them an unfailing provision and discourages the multiplication of the competent and provident by heightening the prospective difficulty of maintaining a family. And thus, in their

eagerness to prevent the really salutory sufferings that surround us, these sigh-wise and groan-foolish people bequeath to posterity a continually increasing curse. (1851, pp.323-4)

It was Social Darwinism mediated through the Eugenics Movement that had a direct effect upon attitudes to the mentally handicapped. The movement systematised and organised the newer attitudes to them and provided a vehicle for conveying these attitudes into a social action programme; it therefore had a profound influence on social policy towards them in the early twentieth century (see below). Galton, the founder of the movemnt, coined the word 'Eugenics' - the science of the improvement of the human race - in 1865 and published in 1869 his study purporting to establish that ability was inherited by demonstrating the high social and economic standing of the forefathers of eminent Victorians. (However, by the end of the century the major influence was non-Spencerian social Darwinism as expounded for example by Karl Pearson. This stressed a collective struggle between groups of men - races - with the fittest group surviving, as opposed to individual economic struggles.) The Eugenics Movement, however, quickly attracted a number of eminent members who began to publish books and articles aimed at doctors and teachers, spelling out the danger that mental defectives posed to society. Among the most influential of these were Down's 'Mental Afflictions of Childhood and Youth' (1887), Beach's 'Treatment and Education of Mentally Feeble Children' (1859), 'Mentally Deficient Children' (1859) by Shuttleworth and Potts, Talbot's 'Degeneracy' (1898) and Ireland's 'Mental Afflictions of Children' (1898).

In the early twentieth century, when botanists brought to light and verified the long-forgotten Mendelian principle of heredity, it was applied by some eugenicists to the transmission of human characteristics including intelligence. (In fact it resulted in a split between the biometricians - who inluded Galton and Darwin and emphasised the blending of parental traits in the offspring - and the Mendelians, who emphasised the particulate nature of heredity.) However, it was not the mode of inheritance that was crucial; rather it was the 'fact' that mental subnormality was inherited at all which influenced the programmes of the Eugenics Movement. The wide acceptance of this principle by the end of the nineteenth century set the stage for and legitimised Eugenic solutions to the 'problem of mental handicap' which were already being put into practice.

The Twentieth Century: The Fear Continues

The social attitudes that began to gain momentum in the late nineteenth century, in both Britain and the United States, continued into the twentieth century and became more widely distributed. The views of the Eugenics Movement came to dominate attitudes towards the mentally handicapped and continued to do so until the 1930s. A firm conviction developed that the retarded could not be trained to be productive members of society and that as well as being a burden on society they were also a social menace, posing a constant threat to civilisation. Society had therefore to be protected from them, and four different policies were advocated at one time or another in Britain and the United States — marriage regulation, birth control, sterilisation and segregation. It quickly became accepted that the 'best solution' was life-long segregation; this not only prevented breeding but also protected the community from current degenerates. The most feared group were the newly discovered 'feebleminded', the mildly subnormal.

Three developments in genetics strengthened the case put forward by the Eugenics Movement. First, the rediscovery of Mendel's laws enabled geneticists to make accurate predictions, sometimes, about the relative proportions of type of offspring to be expected from different kinds of mating. The related belief that most, if not all, traits are determined simply by single genes acting independently, appeared to 'simplify the calculations' and suggest a real possibility that the human race could be improved by selective breeding. Thirdly, the acceptance after 1900 of Weissman's evidence that environmentally acquired characteristics cannot be passed on to offspring entailed his conclusion that all inherited traits are passed on by 'determinants' residing in the germ plasm. This theory was wrongly aplied by many to justify a denial that any possible improvement could be engendered in the defective by manipulation of their environment.

'Scientific proof' of the laws of inheritance of intelligence and degeneracy was provided by the family studies which were undertaken, mainly in the United States, in the last part of the nineteenth century and well into the twentieth century. These studies purported to demonstrate that not only was feeblemindedness inherited (that is, ran in blood-lines as do haemophilia, eye colour and blood group) but also that it was closely associated with criminal behaviour, alcoholism, immorality, pauperism and vagrancy. Degenerates, it was also discovered, tended to have large families, and this added to the fears of the dilution of national intelligence. In the United States, Barr (1904) analysed 3,050 cases to determine the relative contribution of heredity and environment and argued that

hereditary causes, whether acting singly or in combination, are found to be most pronounced ... Furthermore, the influence of some congenital causes is frequently traceable in many of the accidental and developmental causes attributed.
(p.123)

Barr also contended that:

We have surely found evidence in support of the theory that the transmission of imbecility is at once the most insidious and the most aggressive of degenerative forces, attacking alike the physical, mental and moral nature, enfeebling the judgement and the will, while exaggerating the sexual impulses and the perpetuation of an evil growth, a growth too often parasitic, ready to unite with any neurosis it may encounter and from its very sluggishness and inertia refusing to be shaken off ... seen to reappear ... through a century to the fourth or fifth generation.
(p.102)

(The belief in exaggeration of the sexual impulses has passed firmly into the current popular stereotype.) In Britain, Auden, Medical Superintendent for Birmingham, noticed in 1908 when studying the families of mentally defective children that

it is clear that family records such as these point a moral which cannot be permanently disregarded ... society must protect itself from the unrestricted propagation of tainted stock.
(Auden, 1909, p.76)

Probably the most influential study of inherited degeneracy in blood lines was Goddard's study of the Kallikak family. Goddard studied the family backgrounds of the children admitted to the Vineland Institution

23

in the United States where he was Medical Superintendent. He prepared charts whih he claimed 'proved' that feeblemindedness was inherited and closely associated with all types of moral degeneracy, although he recognised, as did the other 'hereditarians', that some forms of mental subnormality were not inherited. However, these latter types usually resulted in severe subnormality and were equally likely to be found among the children of middle and working class parents, whereas feeblemindedness (mild subnormality) was found among the lower working class and closely associated with other social degeneracies. The study of the Kallikaks was published in 1912 and was very influential in England as well as the United States. The study traced the descendents of Martin Kallikak both from a pre-marital liaison with a girl who Goddard claims was feebleminded and from his legal marriage. The genealogical chart demonstrated

> ... the line of descent of the Kallikak family from their
> first colonial ancestors. It was Martin who divided it
> into a bad branch on the one hand and a good branch on the
> other. Each of these branches is traced through the line
> of the eldest son down to a person of the present
> generation. On the bad side it ends with Deborah Kallikak,
> an inmate of the Training School at Vineland, on the good
> side with the son of a prominent and wealthy citizen of the
> same family, now a resident of another state.

Goddard maintained that Martin Jr, the son of the pre-marital liaison, had four hundred and eighty descendents, of whom one hundred and forty-three were mentally deficient and only forty-eight definitely normal, the rest being either unknown or doubtful, although thirty-six were illegitimate, thirty-three sexually promiscuous, twenty-four alcoholics, three epileptics, three criminal, eight kept 'houses of ill fame' and eighty-three died in infancy. In contrast, the descendents of Martin's lawful marriage, who totalled four hundred and ninety-six, all became good, reputable citizens, including doctors, lawyers, judges and other community leaders.

This study was widely regarded as conclusive proof that feeblemindednss was hereditary. Its conclusions were supported by other studies including Estabrook's study of the Wans and Davenport's Hill Folk. The fears of the Eugenics Movement were fuelled by these findings and added to the 'belief' that the feebleminded posed a threat to civilisation.

For many generations we have recognised and pitied the idiot. Of late we have recognised a higher type of defective, the moron and have discovered that he is a burden, that he is a menace to society and civilisation, that he is responsible in a large measure, for many, if not all, of our social problems....

Degeneracy is thus a cancerous blight, constantly spreading tainting and spoiling sound stocks, destroying race values and increasing social burdens.

In fact degeneracy not only handicaps society but threatens its very existence. Congenitally incapable of adjusting themselves to an advanced social order, the degenerate becomes its enemy – particularly the high grade defectives, who are natural fermenters of social unrest.

(Goddard, 1915)

The brief reminiscence of the earlier 'fear of the mob' in this last sentence is not typical of the period, however. More typical is the fear of the feebleminded women expressed by Fernald (1912):

Feebleminded women are almost invariably immoral and if at large usually become carriers of venereal disease or give birth to children who are as defective as themselves. The feebleminded woman who marries is twice as prolific as the normal woman.

The growing concern about the mentally handicapped must, however, be seen in the context of a change in attitudes to the social residuum in the early twentieth century and general fears concerning deterioration of the race. The Boer War had revealed that there was widespread physical disability among the working class, and this led to a re-examination of the old assumptions about the inevitable superiority of the British social system and of the British race. The concern over physical deterioration gave impetus to the political movement for national efficiency and resulted in the advocacy of social reform – although laissez faire continued to be influential, and in practice reforms were very limited and stress continued to be placed on self-help and individual responsibility. It was argued that human resources were being wasted and that the declining birth rate among the

25

upper, middle and respectable working classes, while the residuum was still breeding at a high rate, meant that there would be a deterioration in the race. In America, similarly, there was concern that the quality of the 'national stock' was deteriorating not only because of the supposed differential birth rate – that the 'unfit' were propagating at a faster rate than the 'fit' – but also because institutions such as education, charity and medicine were interfering with natural selection by allowing the unfit to survive.

Many of the same people who advocated social reform and welfare benefits for the poor (with limited success) also accepted the argument that the race was deteriorating because of the diferential fertility of the reputable classes and the residuum. This belief continued despite the fact that the 1903 Inter-departmental Committee on Physical Deterioration found no proof that the race was deteriorating, although they did find that there was widespread poverty, malnutrition and disease. The response to this in Britain, in terms of state education, was twofold. In legislative terms, a limited number of measures were introduced designed to improve the physical fitness of children and working men – the Education (provision of Meals) Act 1906, the Education (Administrative Provisions) Act 1907 which introduced medical inspection into schools, and the National Insurance Act 1911. At the same time the state was strongly encouraging the activities of health visitorss ('teaching' mothers how to raise their babies) and emphasising the desirability of breastfeeding, of the use of 'clean' milk if breastfeeding was not possible, and of mothers withdrawing from paid employment. In other words, the major emphasis in terms of 'improving the stock' was on the importance of 'good mothering' rather than on state policies to reduce poverty, improve housing and so on. This was at least in part because hereditarians dominated the debate after the publication of the Committee's report (see Weeks, 1981) and the continuing influence of laissez faire policies.

The strong influence of Social Darwinism and the fear of the residuum meant that people looked to the biological science to solve the problem of the feeble-minded, however, and the arguments of the Eugenics Movement became very powerful. There was a general consensus among political parties tht the residuum posed a threat and that degeneracy was hereditary. Consequently liberal and Fabian politicians as well as conservative ones advocated eugenic solutions – although

26

there was no complete consensus over this, and considerable disagreement as to whether positive eugenics or negative ones should be employed. Beveridge, who played a vital role in formulating Liberal Party policy in the Edwardian period, justified segregation policies thus:

> The ideal should not be an industrial system arranged with a view to finding room in it for everyone who deserves to enter, but an industrial system in which everyone who did find a place at all should obtain average earnings at least up to the standard of healthy subsistence ... The line between independence and dependence, between the efficient and the unemployable, has to be made clearer and clearer ... the men who through general defects are unable to fill such a whole place in industry are to be recognised as unemployable. They must become the acknowledged dependents of the state, removed from free industry and maintained adequately in public institutions but with a complete and permanent loss of all citizen rights, including not only the franchise but civil freedom and fatherhood.
> (1906)

Pearson (1905) and Sydney Webb (1906) both argued that as the proliferation of untalented and malformed children continued, while the intelligent and well-fed failed to reproduce themselves, no amount of reform aimed at clearing up the slums would improve the general condition of the race. What was necessary was state action in favour of the respectable working class and the talented classes - that is, a programme of positive eugenics - possibly coupled with negative eugenic measures, as the only solution to the problem.

The general consensus over the arguments and policies of the Eugenics Movement (at least in academic and political circles) is shown by the fact that Bertrand Russell not only shared their views concerning the possible deterioration of the race but also felt that negative eugenics were desirable for the mentally defective:

> It must be admitted ... that there are certain dangers. Before long the population may actually diminish ... and government opposition to birth control propaganda gives a

27

> biological advantage to stupidity, since it is chiefly
> stupid people whom governments succeed in keeping in
> ignorance

and

> We may perhaps assume ... governments will acquire the
> right to sterilise those who are not considered desirable
> as parents. This power will be used at first to diminish
> imbecility, a most desirable objective.

The general consensus over the need to prevent the mental deterioration
of the race was based on an acceptance of the 'scientific facts':

> That the physically and mentally fitter stocks produce
> physically and mentally fitter offspring

and that

> Ability not entirely, but largely, runs in stocks and these
> stocks by a long process of social evolution form in bulk
> the upper classes.
> (1924, pp.47-9)

In both Britain and the United States the leading eugenicists were
mostly members of the professional middle classes and in part concerned
with the achievement of a meritocratic society. They favoured state
intervention to prevent the unfit breeding (while, paradoxically,
arguing at the same time that it was state interference (ie social
policy) that caused the problem in the first place by enabling the
'unfit' to breed at such a prolific rate). Nonetheless the Eugenics
Movement in Britain achieved considerable support among socialists.
This strange situation was possible for two major reasons. One was
that the ideology of eugenics was pluralistic: while the majority of
its advocates were anti-environmentalist (Pearson, for example, put the
influence of the environment at a scant tenth), some were able to argue
that the environment would be able to exert due influence only in a
socialist society in which resources were fairly and efficiently
advocated. Secondly, both hereditarians and socialist
environmentalists were concerned to advocate a professionally
administered society and thus found they had interests in common.
Hence the unlikely association of several leading Fabians, for example,
with the more conservative proponents of Eugenics.

The development of intelligence tests in the early part of the
twentieth century provided a 'scientific' method of diagnosing mental

subnormality. Intelligence tests were based on the view that ability was inherited and fixed or at least relatively fixed for life. Mental subnormality, especially feeblemindedness, was seen to be the result of hereditary factors, the inheritance of 'poor' intelligence genes.

... there are laws of inheritance of general mental ability that can be sharply expressed; low mental ability is due to the absence of some factor and if this factor, that determines mental development, is lacking in both parents it will be lacking in all their offspring.

(Davenport, 1911)

The Eugenics Movement and specifically the Eugenics Education Society in Britain (founded in 1907) stressed the need to develop diagnostic techniques to ensure the accurate identification of the mentally defective. They argued that there was no doubt that subnormality was inherited and that society needed to be protected from degeneracy. Auden, a eugenicist, a prominent member of the British Association and Medical Superintendent for Birmingham, emphasised in his 1911 and 1912 reports the need for accurate intelligence tests.

In the case of the feebleminded there is a general diminution of the general intellectual faculties ... the object of the mental test employed should be to measure not so much the intellectual acquisition already made as the inborn all-round efficiency which we have described under the term 'general intelligence'.

(1912, p.64)

In 1911 Newman had advocated the use of intelligence tests to diagnose defectives in his annual report of the Board of Education. An article by Burt in the Eugenics Review in 1913 made it clear that his own growing interest in intelligence testing was dominated largely by the problem of the mentally handicapped — quoting the work of Galton and the recommendation of the 1908 report, he stressed that 'there is no such thing as manufactured feeblemindedness' and that

the fact of mental inheritance can no longer be contested, its importance scarcely overestimated ... there assuredly can be no problem upon which experimentalists, statisticians and psychologists could so fruitfully concentrate their wisdom as the problem of heredity and its influence upon the mind.

(Burt, 1913, p.183)

Thus in Britain and America in the early part of the twentieth century there was some general agreement that the mentally handicapped presented a menace to society and that they could be identified reliably and objectively by scientific means. There was a fair measure of agreement also on the solution to the problem:

> We have seen that lifelong care is essential and that the most forcible argument in its favour is that every feebleminded person who is not under restraint is a menace to the community: not only is such an individual very likely to become a so-called criminal, drunkard or prostitute but also he or she may propagate and spread a taint that is wholly bad by having children, legitimate or illegitimate.
>
> (Lapage, 1920, p.197)

Views such as this were widely expressed in medical and psychological works and in the other writings of members of the Eugenics Movement. It is of course difficult to determine how deeply these views and attitudes penetrated into 'everyday consciousness' but many of the common stereotypes and fears can be seen to be underpinned by them. Indeed, the only notable success of the Eugenics movement was the Mental Health Act 1913; they did not succeed in promulgating positive eugenic measures, and it was only with regard to mental degeneration – feeblemindednesss – that they had any major political influence. What is more important, however, is that they succeeded in constructing and imposing a new 'discourse' of mental handicap which still underpins popular attitudes today. (One should not lose sight, however, of the material circumstances which supported the views and policies – the existence of an economic system of relation which could not afford to have any section of the populace seen as not involved in it and which depeded for its continued existence, as it still does, on the continued value of its main basic resource of labour.)

The official policy of confinement in Britain

The changing conception of the mentally subnormal in the early twentieth century was quickly reflected in social policy. The growing concern about the problems presented by, and the danger of, the mentally subnormal resulted in British government setting up a Royal Commission in 1904. (Indeed, the publication of the Commission's findings was in its turn one of the major factors in the growth of fear of the feebleminded in Britain and America.) The Commission's terms of reference were 'to consider the existing methods of dealing with idiots and epileptics and with imbeciles, feebleminded or defective persons not certified within the lunacy laws' and to recommend an amendent of the law and other measures to protect the community from danger and hardship, 'due regard being had to the expense ... and to the best means of securing economy'. Set up under the chairmanship of H.J. Gladstone, the Commission started receiving evidence in 1904 and published its results in June of 1908, after examining submissions from inspectors and medical officers of special schools, reformatories, prisons, lunatic and idiot asylums, as well as representatives of other groups deemed able to give information. They also surveyed methods of handling in the United States, Europe, Ireland and Scotland.

The report expressed considerable concern about the existing provision made for the mentally subnormal, especially in view of the size of the problem (it was estimated that at least one in two hundred and seventeen, ie 0.46 per cent of the population was mentally defective and that at least one in one hundred and twenty-seven, ie 0.79 per cent, of school children were either idiots, imbeciles or feebleminded) and of the fact that they needed to be adequately controlled in order to protect society.

> Of the gravity of the present state of things, there is no doubt ... there are numbers of mentally defective persons whose training is neglected, over whom no sufficient control is exercised and whose wayward and irresponsible lives are productive of crime and misery, of much injury to themselves and to others and of much continuous expenditure wasteful to the community and the individual family.
> (volume 8, p.8)

Considerable concern was expressed about all the mentally defective, but one group, the feebleminded, were selected out as needing special attention. Many of the feebleminded were not properly trained, according to the report, and as a consequence became criminals, paupers or members of other social problem groups. This meant that they placed an intolerable social and economic burden on the community. Evidence was presented by doctors and medical officers that the feebleminded were inclined to breed at an alarming rate. Tredgold, for example, pointed out that while the average number of children born to 'normal' parents was four, the 'degenerate families' averaged 7.3; the Royal Commission accepted this evidence.

The perceived dangers of mentally defective people led expert witnesses – such as Sir W Chance and Dr M Cooke to advocate their life-long segregation. Miss Denby of the Association for the Permanent Care of the Feebleminded also pointed to the 'dangers' of leaving mentally subnormal children in the community. The Royal Commission concluded:

> ... we have pointed out how strong is the argument for the detention of the mentally defective in suitable institutions ... segregation and control should follow immediately on their leaving a special class ... The evidence ... emphasises the necessity of segregation or detention on the widest grounds of public policy.

The recommendations of the report reflected very clearly three current concepts concerning the nature and extent of mental deficiency. They felt that society needed to be protected from the mentally deficient and that considerable efforts needed to be made to identify all mental defectives. While in general the mental defectives should be segregated in hospitals, asylums or colonies, it was felt that in a few cases family care or guardianship orders would suffice. (Sterilisation was considered but rejected; although cheap, it was felt that it would offend public opinion – see volume 2, p.97.)

The report received a very mixed reception. In particular the Eugenics Movement, especially the Eugenics Education Society, did not feel that the recommendations went far enough if society was to be protected from the subnormal. As a result the government decided not to introduce legislation immediately but to await further developments.

Two powerful pressure groups – the Eugenics Education Society and the National Association for the Permanent Care of the Feebleminded – launched a campaign to keep the public informed of the importance of the eugenic problem and to persuade the government to introduce legislation enforcing the permanent care and segregation of the mentally defective. Tredgold lobbied MPs to propagate the idea that mental deficiency was hereditary and was leading to the dgeneracy of the race. Galton and Montague Crackenthorpe (first President of the EES) used the columns of 'The Times' to argue the hereditarian case, while Auden, co-founder of the Birmingham branch of the EES, emphasised the problem of racial decay in one of his earliest reports. In 1910 Miss Pissent (quoted in Jones, 1972, p 197) advocated the permanent care of the feebleminded in a speech made to a church congress. She justified this policy by referring to the American Family Studies and giving examples of families in England who despite considerable social work support were too defective to care adequately for their families. Moreover, the Minority Report of the Poor Law Commission firmly linked mental deficiency to pauperism:

> In the United Kingdom the mentally deficient number in all
> their grades more than one sixth of the entire pauper list
> — and many approaching two hundred thousand in number
> constantly requiring maintenance from the rates.
> (p.891)

The work of these two pressure groups aroused public opinion and considerable concern was expressed about the 'danger' that defectives posed to ordinary citizens and to the community. By 1912 the Home Office had received more than eight hundred resolutions from public bodies, advocating the permanent care and segregation of the mentally defective, including the feebleminded. The submission of resolutions by public bodies does not of course 'prove' that public opinion was aroused; it does, however, show that there was some general concern. Councils and Education Authorities are elected bodies and they reflect to some extent the concerns of the local electorate, or at least what they feel concerns the local electorate. It is of course likely that only a few vocal and influential citizens expressed 'real' concern and that this coupled with newspaper campaigns and the work of the two pressure groups both supported by leading and influential figures, created a 'moral panic', the 'man in the street' being considerably influenced by the media, and official views and fear being widely disseminated.

As a result of this pressure two Bills which incorporated the eugenicist assumptions were introduced in 1912, one by M.G. Stewart MP and one by the Home Secretary. Both passed the Second Reading and were referred to Standing Committee. After several postponements the latter Bill was reintroduced in March 1913 and received the Royal Assent on August 15, 1913. The delays occurred because the Bill was widely attacked both in and outside Parliament. Four newspapers, 'The Citizen', the 'Daily News', the 'Daily Herald' and the 'Manchester Guardian', all criticised. The fears of the Bill's opponents were expressed in Parliament by, among others, the Conservative MP Robert Cecil, who justified his concern thus:

> I confess I feel very nervous about applying any remedy on
> the grounds of eugenics in the present condition of our
> knowledge of that science.
> (Hansard, 1907; 1912, pp.721-38)

It was felt that the Bill went too far in its recommendations and despite a campaign in 'The Times' by supporters the government withdrew it.

The withdrawal of the Bill immediately led to a campaign for its reintroduction, in the media and from pressure groups and powerful citizens. Articles appeared in the 'Lancet' in support of the Bill.

> We live in days when even the most sentimental
> humanitarians can hardly be blind to the fact that for
> nations, as for individuals, the struggle for existence is
> still a stern reality and that in the struggle,efficiency
> is the price of survival ... It is a lesson which is
> applicable to other matters beside the propagation and
> conduct of war and nowhere is it more pertinent than in
> what to do with the furthering of racial fitness.
> (14.19.1912)

A new Bill was introduced in 1913, which left out the most controversial clauses in the previous one – the clause forbidding marriage and the one permitting compulsory sterilisation. Parliamentary opposition virtually disappeared, the official opposition agreeing not to oppose the Bill. The only effective opposition came from a few back benchers. One of these, Wedgewood, pointed to the class nature of the Bill and argued that it was aimed at social control and at improving the wealth-producing power of the working class, by incarcerating those who were not able to work at the required level. The measures in the Bill were not aimed at all the mentally subnormal, but only at the 'feebleminded', who came from deprived working class backgrounds. But these few voices raised in opposition were hardly heard in the hurry to get it through Parliament and on the Statute Book as quickly as possible.

The 1913 Mental Health Act incorporated the main recommendations of the Royal Commission and also reflected the concern that had been expressed about the inadequacies of some of the conclusions of the report. Four classes of people were defined as coming within the terms of the Act: idiots, imbeciles, the feebleminded and 'moral defectives'. The Act set up a Central Board of Control and required County and County Borough Councils to ascertain the numbers of mental defectives in their area and to provide and maintain sufficient institutions to 'care' for them. Local Education Authorities were required to report all children over seven years old who were ineducable and were responsible for informing the Local Authority of those leaving special schools who required supervision. Legal requirements were laid down governing the reception and detention of mentally defective persons. Feebleminded families giving birth to illegitimate children, habitual drunkards, vagrants, criminals, feebleminded minors (ie those under twenty-one years) and imbeciles and idiots of any age could be compulsorily detained. Mental deficiency had to be diagnosed by two doctors; once diagnosed an individual could be detained indefinitely, although provision was made for periodic review of the condition of those detained under the Act. Local Authorities were empowered to put mentally handicapped individuals under guardianship orders in the community, although the provision was not widely used. (The Act provided little or no legal safeguard for the diagnosed individuals, so that many individuals were wrongly detained under it for many years or even for life – see NCCL, 1951.) In summary, the Act formally laid down the principle of making special provision for the mentally subnormal, identified them as a specific problem group and gave wide powers of detention. It also marked them out as a group incapable of supporting themselves, a burden on the community to be permanently hidden away. They were stigmatised as not fully human in a society where 'humanity' implies the ability to be economically and socially productive and a man's worth is measured by his ability to secure and hold down a job.

Although now 'brought to official notice', the retarded continued in many ways to be ignored. Many Local Authorities were slow to implement the provisions of the Act. By 1927 Local Authorities still only provided 5,301 beds for the mentally handicapped, although the number of ascertained 'defectives' was over 60,000. This seems to have been due to the cost of providing permanent segregation and suggests that public concern about the 'danger' of the mentally handicapped may not have been as great as that of government, a few influential public figures and the Eugenics Movement.

> It is difficult to convince members of the council that the expense of maintaining the feebleminded who cannot maintain themselves must eventually be born by the community and that it is a choice between maintenance under improper conditions in Poor Law Institutions, in provision by outdoor relief or unemployment benefit, or maintenance in institutions where they are under continuous training and care.
> (Board of Control, 1927)

The Board also suggested that mental defectives were a source of danger to neighbours and the community generally and that for this reason it was essential to detain them for life in asylums.

As it became evident that the 1913 Act was not being fully implemented, the government decided to set up a committee in 1926 to investigate the current situation with respect to children. The terms of reference of the committee were later extended to include adults. The Wood Committee reported in 1929. It made its recommendations within a conception of mental deficiency that regarded it still as a social and a genetic problem. Mental defectives were seen as the last stage of the inheritancy of degeneracy – the degenerate group making up at least ten per cent of the population. Particular concern was expressed about mental defectives of the primary amentic type, and it was argued that if all the families of mental defectives of this type were collected together

> It would include ... a much larger proportion of insane persons, epileptics, paupers, criminals (especially recidivists), unemployables, habitual slum dwellers,

36

prostitutes, inebriates and other social inefficients than would a group of families not containing mental defectives.
(part III)

An epidemological survey carried out for the committee estimated that one per cent of the population was mentally deficient; of these, twenty-five per cent were idiots or imbeciles and seventy-five per cent feebleminded. The group seen as the real 'threat' was also the most numerous. The Committee recommended life-long segregation as the only effective means of dealing with the problem. However, recognising the cost of this, they argued that mental deficiency asylums were to be places of detention, not hospitals. The Wood Committee did not go to the extreme of recommending sterilisation as a solution, as had happened in the United States. In 1933, however, the Brock Committee did recommend voluntary sterilisation for the mentally defective, not because they felt that it would solve the 'problem' of mental deficiency but that it might check the growth of a spreading group of people who were not wanted by their parents or anybody else.

The Brock Committee also recommended improved care for mental defectives as well as he provision of training and productive work for those detained in asylums. The economic situation of the depression meant that there was little headway made in the provision of intitutions, although by 1937 eighty-one Local Authorities in England and Wales out of one hundred and twenty-three were making provision for the accommodation of the mentally defective (PEP, 1937). There was instead a turn to community care as the solution, 'policy' slowly becoming that mentally subnormal people should be cared for in the community rather than incarcerated in institutions.

The move towards the community

By the 1930s it was beginning slowly to be recognised that the mentally handicapped might not pose quite the danger, individually and collectively, that had been supposed. Indeed, by the late 1930s non-custodial care was widely advocated but few facilities were provided and the same attitues often appear to underlie the advocacy; the American Association on Mental Deficiency, for example, argued in 1939 for:

37

the construction of institutions for the feebleminded; a
complete census and registration of all mentally deficient
persons in institutionsl care and training, with a
permanent segregation of those who cannot make satisfactory
social adjustments in the community; parole for all
suitable institutionally trained mentally defective
persons; extra-institutional supervision of all defectives
in the community.

(quoted in the Introduction to Rosen et al, volume 2)

Social policy and attitudes in the United States in the period up to
the Second World War paralleled Britain's. Indeed, both scientific
research and social policy initiatives in America influenced and were
influenced by those of Britain. The dominant policy in both remained
the provision of segregated institutional care. In both, the group
most feared and to whom the greatest attention was paid was that of the
mildy handicapped (referred to as 'feebleminded' in Britain and as
'morons' in the United States). In America as in Britain sterilisation
and the regulation of marriage were considered as alternatives to
life-long segregation. In Britain, sterilisation legislation was never
passed, although it was often advocated. In America twenty-three
states passed such legislation, although in a few it was subsequently
declared unconstitutional.

The dominant policy in the early twentieth century remained
commitment to state-run institutions, but there were never sufficient
places for all those perceived to need custodial care. In America the
state institutes became grossly overcrowded and had long waiting lists,
while many mentally handicapped people continued to be warehoused in
children's homes, county poor farms and almshouses. The picture was
much the same in Britain. The result is well expressed by
Wolfensberger:

Retarded people were congregated into huge groups,
segregated from society, segregated from other retarded
persons of the opposite sex, a-sexualised and dehumanised
in poorly supported, inhumanly run regimented institutions.

However, by the 1930s many professionals were beginning to suggest that
very many mentally handicapped people could be cared for in the
community, and public fear of the degenerate had diminished. Community
studies had demonstrated that many mildly handicapped people could cope

quite adequately, and it was also becoming quite evident that the aims of segregation were not achievable – although prevented from breeding, the retarded were not becoming less numerous in successive generations. In America, as in Britain, large numbers of mentally handicapped people were never institutionalised; many were cared for by their families, with little or no help from the community or the state. It was becoming increasingly apparent, indeed, that a considerable proportion of the mildly handicapped were never identified. Pressure began to build up for a change of policy. It seems relevant to ask, in the same terms as earlier in the paper, what might be seen as underlying the beginnings of this change.

One obvious factor was the cost. In England up to the Second World War there was a constant tension between protecting the public by segregating the mentally handicapped and keeping the cost of providing for them as low as possible – a reflection of the continuing influence of liberal laissez faire ideology and its distrust of state intervention. The 1903 Commission, as we have seen, had economy as part of its terms of reference. In 1910, when advocating life–long segregation, Tredgold had explicitly stated that care should be provided at the minimum expense compatible with adequate supervision. One of the major reasons for advocating sterilisation was cost: if mildly handicapped people – partiularly women – were sterilised, then they could be left in the community without fear of their passing on their 'taint'. It is also evident that one of the factors leading to the advocacy of non–custodial control in the 1930s was the realisation that it was too expensive to provide residential care for all mentally handicapped people – particularly in the economic climate of the time. (This is of course also the reason why community facilities were not provided.) The most explicit expression of the need to keep costs as low as possible may be seen in the development of the farm colonies in the United States; the explicit aim was to reduce per capita cost to the lowest possible level by admitting as many people as possible and by the more functional of the inmates performing useful work on the land or in the institution. (See eg Johnson, 1902; Fernald, 1902; Bernstein, 1920.) As in Britain, few amenities were provided, little provision was made for training or occupation (NCCL, 1951) and the institutions became very large – the largest in the United States held over three thousand inmates.

Cost alone, however, cannot explain what amounts to a partial change of ideology. It is difficult to say precisely what it was that shifted public and general attitudes – the writers of the 1930s and 1940s were often less explicit than those earlier in the century in stating their own ideological presuppositions. Three factors might be advanced as possible determinants, however – listed here in reverse order of probable influence (as it appears to us).

(1) One would like to think that the public learned from the German example – that Hitler's 'final solution' to various perennial problems fostered a distaste for eugenic solutions in general. This was undoubtedly a factor in the late 1940s, after film of the extermination camps had been widely disseminated. There is little evidence from Britain that the German practice was generally known or disapproved in the 1930s, however, and less from America.

(2) A second possible influence may have been the changed economic climate. An ideological insistence of the value of work as a necessity for maintaining a system of economic relations loses some of its force when the work cannot be provided, and the 1920s and 1930s were a time of mass unemployment during which the supposed inability of the retarded to perform productive labour simply put them in the same economic position as many more fortunate in their abilities. Again this seems unlikely as a major determinant of ideology, however: at the time of writing there are over three million unemployed in Britain but a stigma still attaches to unemployment.

(3) The most plausible way of understanding what happened seems paradoxically to be the most fanciful – that the 'general fear' which was originally attached to the riotous and subversive but came to transfer itself to the incapable had begun to move back again to its original target. The 'fear of the mob' was at its original height not very long after the French Revolution, where a government and a system of power-relations had been overthrown by the mob. In 1917 the Russian Revolution achieved a similar result, and there were similar though abortive processes apparent in Europe in the first quarter of the century. The first quarter of the twentieth century saw the foundation of the Cooperative Movement in England, the rise of the Labour Party and (most important) the phenomenal growth of the Trade Union Movement and

of organised labour. In the 1920s the possibility of a General Strike was discussed as a likely precursor to violent revolution — for example, in some of the fictional works of Agatha Christie. It seems not implausible that those aspects of the system of economic relations which most directly influence what appears in the public media — and thus eventually in popular ideology — were themselves influenced to direct their attention towards the more immediate threat of socialised labour. This in turn, would mean that for the mentally handicapped 'the heat was off'.

Whatever the underlying influences, the 'fear' of the feebleminded had receded by the 1930s and largely evaporated by the 1940s. This did not mean that they were handled any differently at first. Many were segregated in overcrowded institutions which housed them but did not train them. Few in institutions were returned to the community, because no facilities existed for them there. By the 1950s, however, pressure for community treatment was becoming very powerful. A report from the British National Council for Civil Liberties in 1951 called the plight of the retarded 'one of the greatest social scandals of the twentieth century' and a World Health Organisation report in 1954 also argued very strongly the need for greater community provision. Over the next thirty years great strides have been made towards making 'community care' a reality; though financial and institutional support still falls pitifully short of what is needed in many cases, nonetheless mental handicap has become a state concern and part of 'normal' state welfare provision.

Thus in the last thirty years the policy of 'community care' has been widely and increasingly advocated in both Britain and the United States, but in terms of practical provision the State's action has been slow and insufficient — as one would expect in response to a 'social problem' class which is now seen as more of a nuisance than a threat. In Britain the Mental Health Act 1959 advocated community care for mentally handicapped people, but the major statement of intent to provide community-based resources did not follow until the 1971 White Paper Better Services for the Mentally Handicapped. More recent government publications have admitted that the White Paper's targets for reduction of numbers in long-stay hospitals have not been met but continued to stress their commitment to community care — which means in practice the transfer of responsibility (and costs) from the NHS to

41

local authority social services. Alternative provision (eg hostel places) has indeed increased, but not nearly at a rate suffciient to meet the actual needs of mentally handicapped people (see eg Norris, 1975), and this is especially the case when we consider that 80 per cent of severely subnormal children, 40 per cent of severely subnormal adults and the vast majority of mildly handicapped people live with relatives or in some form of residence in the community (DHSS, 1978).

Care in the community has meant in practice that the place of residence of mentally handicapped people has changed, but there is little evidence of integration into the community (see Bayley, 1973; Walker, 1981; Abbott, 1982; Finch and Groves, 1983). 'Community' is a portmanteau word, and what 'community care' is actually supposed to mean is often by no means clear. It is evident, however, that advocates of the policy have generally been arguing for more than a relocation of facilities; rather, the suggestion is that mentally handicapped people be enabled to become part of the community and be care for by as well as in the community (see, eg, Bayley, 1973). The Jay Report (DHSS, 1979), indeed, argued that community care was too low an aim and that the target should be 'normalisation' - enabling people to live as normal a life as is compatible with their degree of handicap and to be accepted as full members of the community within which they live. The reality in Britain, however, is very different from this; community care in practice means either care by the family (with the burden falling mostly on a female member) or isolated hostel living.

Why, however, did the move towards community care or normalisation ever become seen as the preferable policy alternative, and accepted by governments? Psychological and sociological research in the 1950s and 1960s strongly suggested that children developed better, both cognitively and emotionally, if cared for in a family environment (Bowlby, 1954; Lyle, 1958, 1959a,b; Tizard, 1964) and that hospitals and other large institutions were dehumanising (Goffman, 1961; King, Raynes and Tizard, 1971; Barton, 1959; Wing and Brown, 1970). Furthermore, the founding of the Welfare State meant that facilities existed in the community ready to be drawn on by mentally handicapped people. Additionally, the policies fitted in with the ideology of welfarism and equality of opportunity that was developing in Britain (see eg Scull, 1977). An important selling point seems also to have been that policies of community care appeared to be a cheap as well as a humanitarian alternative to institutional care.

However, it would seem that organisational needs rather than humanitarian cocnerns have again provided the major impetus behind the acceptance of such policies. In practice 'community care' has meant shifting the major part of the costs from the public purse to the private individual or family. Hospitals have been closed down, but local authority social services departments have not increased their spending to a comparable degree (see Scull, 1977; Abbott, 1982). The importance of financial factors is brought out clearly in recent government reports, where (a) it has been suggested that community care might need to be reconsidered for some groups because it could prove more expensive than residential care, and (b) it is recognised that if the real costs currently born by the family were to fall on the state, then community care would be more expensive than residential care in almost all cases (DHSS, 1981a, 1981b).   In practice a policy of community care for mentally handicapped people has most commonly meant care by the family, with little help from the state (Buckle, 1984). The primary agents of this care are not paid employees of the state, but the mothers of mentally handicapped people. It is to them and the nature of their lives that we turn in the second paper of this collection.

2 'LEAVING IT TO MUM': MOTHERHOOD AND MENTAL HANDICAP

In the last paper we looked at a 'reading' of the history of mental
handicap - one which goes some way towards casting light on the
problems and exeriences which currently form part of the life of
families with mentally handicapped children. On the one hand we were
able to 'explain' the fear and dislike of the mentally handicapped
which forms part of our current 'cultural stock', by locating its
origins in a real and in contemporary eyes national concern for the
'survival of the race', backed by the science of the times. On the
other hand the current policy of treatment - 'community care' - is
shown to have developed by current financial expediency out of the
'need' to protect 'society', and at no point to have grown from the
needs of either the mentally handicapped or their families, despite the
genuine efforts of philanthropists in this cause. The current paper
completes the 'critical circle' by exploring the lived experience of
those most responsible for the care of retarded children - that is,
their mothers - in contrast with the experience of mothers in general.

The policy of 'community care' for mentally handicapped children
has non-financial costs for families: work which in institutions would
be wage-labour becomes unpaid work for 'Mum' when the burden of care is

transferred to the family. This paper looks at the nature and extent of such work and at the extent to which it alters the nature of the mother's life. We look also at the price which is paid by the whole family for the fact of having a mentally handicapped member - a price made up of shattered expectations which have to be rebuilt, the disturbance to family life, the reactions of others, the constraints on the mother's life, and the disturbance of normal expectations for the family's future. (The 'price' differs markedly from family to family, depending at least in part on the degree of handicap, the extent of associated physical handicaps and the social and economic situation of the family; what follows is a composite, not necessarily true to the experience of any one mother.)

The data come from two main sources. One is research which we carried out jointly during 1981 and 1982 in and around a new city in the English midlands, interviewing mothers of mentally handicapped children (and sometimes other family members who happened to be present). Sixteen families were contacted from a list extracted for us from the school rolls of two Special Schools in the new city (one designated for the mildly handicapped and one for the severely). We carried out two interviews with each mother separated by about a year, not using a formal questionnaire but rather trying for the atmosphere of a friendly chat about life and work between neighbours. Although the interviews were tape-recorded, it seemed to us that this atmosphere was readily attained in most cases - the more so because Abbott was very evidently pregnant during the early interviews. This was one main source of our information. The other was a similar series of interviews carried out earlier by Abbott with families in an outer London suburb, contacted through the good offices of the local branch of the National Society for Mental Handicap. Although we cannot claim that either of these small-scale studies has a sample statistically representative of the population of mentally handicapped children, we would claim that together they cover a large part of the range - from the mildest of borderline handicaps to the very severe, and from pre-school children to (in Abbott's study) 'children' in their forties. These data are contrasted with a parallel series of interviews with mothers of children who have not been labelled as mentally handicapped.

Reactions to handicap

One major set of costs to the family of the mentally handicapped child is the reactions which the family will have and will encounter to the fact that their child is handicapped. The family has to come to terms with altered expectations for the child, an altered perspective for the future, and the cultural stigma which attaches to the label. A family 'lifestyle' has to be built which can cope with the situation – and revised, and re-revised as time goes on. Finally, the family has to negotiate its position <u>vis a vis</u> the outside world and to deal with the real, expected or imagined reations of others. This section looks at the price the family pays for its 'abnormal' member and at how family members cope with it.

The initial reaction may vary from grief to outright emotional rejection. On the one hand grief may be immediate and temporarily overwhelming: [The doctor] was rather brutal. I mean true enough one has to learn ... but I left that surgery in tears ... and I walked and I was crying as I walked along.

(Mrs Neade)

Grief may be delayed but no less powerful when it does come: two of the sixteen mothers to whom we spoke described long periods (in one case two or three years) of numbness, followed by some kind of breakdown. For others again there may be a period during which the child is effectively rejected:

For about a month after I found out I didn't have any feeling for her any way – she wasn't my baby, she was just a baby that had got to be looked after and fed and kept clean. I couldn't pick her up and cuddle her or nothing ... And I walked past the pram one day and she looked up at me and she smiled at me ... she just smiled ... after that I was all right.

(Mrs Miller)

Immediate expectations are broken, and there may be disappointment and jealousy:

Four girls, five girls who I went to school with .. all had beautiful bouncing babies, and there was me with my poor little thing. I was a bit resentful.

(Mrs Miller)

> I was most disappointed, because I thought I was
> going to have a beautiful-looking baby, you know. Well,
> she was all colours, she was bleeding all over.
> (Mrs King)

Immediate decisions have to be taken: to take the child home or to leave 'it' in the hospital, to seek or not to seek institutionalisation after the child has gone home, to take all the small decisions which may appear to happen automatically - 'It's just part of something that happens and you just get on with it ... you don't think about each day, do you?' - but which amount to a commitment to care in the community. The beginnings of a stance towards the outside world have also to be adopted: for example, the decision not to attempt concealment:

> the sooner people knew, I thought, the nicer for them,
> because there's nothing worse than looking in a pram and
> it's a friend, and thinking, 'Oh goodness, what can I say?'
> (Mrs Rushden)

Thus the first thing that has to be done by the family is to come to terms with broken expectations and altered circumstances - to do the hard work of building the beginnings of the new and different life. At this time there may also have to be a reassessment of self. Whether or not the feeling is judged irrational, there may be a denigration of self - 'I felt inadequate, I felt it must be me' (Mrs Miller) - and a need to construct some answer to the question 'Why me?'. Seven of our sixteen mothers mentioned some kind of 'hereditary taint' as something for which one or the other side of the family needed to take some blame - a survival in popular consciousness of the outdated science of the Eugenics Movement - and three others denied a belief in heredity with enough vehemence that one suspects the question had been an issue for the family. Fathers also may have to come to terms with 'being the sort of person' who has produced a mentally handicapped child - self-labelling can run all the more rampant because this is an area of life where it is difficult for spouses even to talk to each other, let alone talk to others outside the family - and siblings may worry about themselves and have their worries reinforced by their school friends.

All of the mothers in our new city sample had made some kind of initial working adjustment, but the same was not true of all of their husbands. Three of the sixteen marriages broke up after the birth of the handicapped child - not solely because of the child's handicap, but

48

at least in part because the husband could not accept it - and in another case the marriage was put under great strain. Most of the husbands of the women we have interviewed are described by their wives as having difficulty in coming to terms with themselves and their children, and in general it is found that stress similar in degree to the mothers but different in kind (less self-punitive, on the whole) may be detected in most fathers of mentally handicapped children (Cummings, 1976). Husbands sometimes have to change their lifestyle radically in order to facilitate the adjustment of the family. Sometimes the husband's job or career has to be modified: for example, one man in our new city sample gave up several chances of promotion to save moving to another area, and another took on a fish and chip shop, with his wife, in order to be more available to the family. Substantial reorganisation of normally expected roles may be necessary to preserve an otherwise normal family life: siblings may have to take on a parental role with respect to the handicapped child, and the husband may have to play more of a part in family life than is the norm.

The literature suggests that on the whole fathers become more involved in child care than those whose children are not mentally handicapped. In a survey carried out by Hunter (1980), for example, 25 per cent of employed fathers of mentally handicapped children were 'on nights' or on shift work, and therefore available to take children to clinics and in general to look after them during the day; some fathers had changed to shift work precisely for this reason. On the other hand, some studies find the opposite: Gallagher et al (1983), for example, note that 'the father often plays a limited role in these families even when present'. Both in our new city sample and in the earlier South London work the predominent experience was nearer to the latter state than the former - fathers did help with children, but in general no more so than might be found in some other families. The immediate stress of handicap is in any case less for employed fathers than for non-working mothers because they escape from home for substantial periods of the day. The relationship between husband and wife may well deteriorate nonetheless, as we have seen.

Thus one major 'price' which the parents of mentally handicapped children have to pay for their children is a reorganisation of how the family sees itself and how life is lived within it and in interaction

49

with others around it. A second, related price is paid in terms of the nature of the family's identity vis a vis the outside world and the consequent reactions of others. Mental handicap is a stigmatising condition in our culture, and it is not only the retarded themselves who carry the stigma, but also their families. Goffman (1963) refers to the sharing of another's spoilt identity as 'bearing a courtesy stigma' – the family members have a spoilt identity because of their close affiliation to someone who bears the primary signs. Birenbaum (1970) suggests that the families of the mentally subnormal tend to provide a very good example of a group of people who carry this kind of courtesy stigma but who seek to maintain a normal appearance by carrying on with the 'normal' life pattern. In order to do this they maintain a 'normal' family life, avoid stigmatising situations and retain social relationships. Sometimes this may mean a dramatic change in the nature of the social relations which are retained. The South London sample, for instance, were all active members of their local Association and tended to use it as a basis for the family's social life. This was much less common among our later new city sample – the local Association was far less active there – but many of the mothers at least were actively involved with the teachers and social workers of the ESN(S) school or with the newly formed parents' association at the ESN(M) school. Several mothers were also active in charitable work for the mentally handicapped – Mrs Neade, for example, had until recently been a local organiser for Home Farm Trust's fund-raising activities, and Mrs Rushden was involved in so many things that she described mental handicap as her hobby. While some were well integrated in villages or urban communities, and others in a state of 'normal' urban isolation, others tended to shape their friendships around their retarded children. In Mrs Ovenden's words,

I miss my friends. Nearly all my friends now are mothers who have children with difficulties, from the [ESN(M)] school, and they've been a great help. But some of the others! One woman kept trying to put Clive down by getting her own child (the same age) to show him how to do things. He doesn't worry, of course, but I mind ...

In any case the problem of integration tends to become greater as the child reaches adulthood and it becomes increasingly difficult to retain an appearance of normality.

The experiences of the eleven families interviewed in the South London study varied considerably. Some felt intensely that they were stigmatised as a consequence of having a handicapped member and that other people openly displayed negative reactions towards them. These negative reactions might be displayed by relatives, friends, the 'general public' and professionals alike. Conversely others felt that everyone had been very helpful and kind. Abbott's own impressions - from looks, inflections in the voice and other cues as well as from what people said - were that they had all had disturbing experiences and that they all felt that other peple regarded them as 'different', pitied them and to some extent avoided them. Also they all seemed to structure their lives as families so as to avoid possibly embarrasing situations - for example, by not asking friends to babysit, by not inviting friends or relatives to call who they felt would be embarrassed by the presence of the subnormal member. What came over most clearly was a feeling that people's attitudes were ambivalent: that at an abstract level they experienced sympathy but that when confronted with the possibility of direct contact with the mentally handicapped they tried to avoid it. Out new city data would admit of a similar analysis.

One has to remember that the majority of people have no first-hand knowledge of the mentally handicapped. They have stereotyped images, often influenced by outdated 'scientific' knowledge and occasionally stirred up by sensationalised newspaper articles. (Attitudes towards sex and the mentally handicapped, discussed below, are a good example of this tendency.) These images more often refer to the severely thar. to the mildly subnormal. Shearer (1972), for example, has suggested that

it is still widely believed that mentally handicapped people are uncontrolled and perverted in their sexual appetites. In the past this belief has been one of the main incentives for shutting them away in segregated institutions.

(p 3)

and Greengrass (1976) that

the fearful myth that the mentally sick and subnormal ... are promiscuous and have voracious sexual appetites which they are incapable of satisfying responsibly or within a

51

socially acceptable pattern of behaviour is one that still
holds water for many, and although statistics keep pouring
out to explode the myth, old prejudices and fears die hard
(p.94)

This would seem to be a good example of how arguments developed by the
Eugenics Movement and others to justify the permanent segregation of
mentally handicapped people have filtered through and still influence
people's perceptions of the mentally handicapped. The 'outdated' views
referred to in the above quotations were clearly expressed in books and
articles on the mentally subnormal in the first two decades of this
century. However, the view that at least some mentally subnormal men
and women have abnormal appetites is still openly stated by 'experts'.
Tredgold and Soddy's influential textbook for the medical profession
argued as recently as 1970 that in the case of subnormal men

open masturbation in the presence of others, indecent
exposure, indecent assault especially on immature girls,
occasional rape and sexual murder are possible
(p.90)

while in the case of

subnormal girls ... in some ways the problems ... are even
more intractable ... Some subnormal girls have
comparatively strong direct sex drives ... The
gratification aspects of their sexuality will be uppermost.
Some girls will discover how to use their bodies to give
them power over men and drift into prostitution ... The
self-gratification aspects of their need can also drive
girls into sexual promiscuity.
(p.91)

(There is indeed some evidence that mentally handicapped men commit
more than their fair share of sexual offences, and that although they
are not very often violent their victims are often young children.
However, the total numbers of mentally handicapped men charged and
convicted of such offences are very small - see Walker and McCabe,
1973.)

While scientific and social developments in the twentieth century
have resulted in changes in the way the mentally handicapped are
conceptualised and in methods of handling, nonetheless the beliefs of
the Eugenics Movement live on to a large extent in 'popular

52

consciousness'. The prevalence and power of the stereotype is well illustrated by a study described by one of us (Abbott, 1982) of a village's reactions to the establishment of a hostel for mentally handicapped women. While many of the villagers objected vociferously to the hostel and expressed fears for the safety of the village's children, what was most revealing was the ambivalent attitudes of a group who became 'Friends of the Hostel' and visited the girls regularly. Even these women had doubts about whether the hostel should have been opened in their village and in fact shared many of the fears that they claimed were voiced by those opposed to the hostel - fears of violent and sexually uncontrolled behaviour. Similar attitudes and prejudices emerged in group dicussions which Abbott ran with full-time students in a college of further education, a generation on from the 'Friends of the Hostel' and a group selected as of sufficient academic ability to cope with GCE 'O' and 'A' levels. The majority of these students showed no knowledge of mental handicap, had obviously never thought about it, and held views and expectations obviously based on the most extreme and bizarre degrees of subnormality. They expected that their parents would react adversely to the foundation of a hostel in their area, and justified this attitude by the supposed danger the mentally handicapped present to children and old people. Confusion between the mentally handicapped and the mentally ill was also very common.

Ignorance and prejudice are not confined to the populace at large but may readily penetrate the kin group. One of the South London families, for example, expressed a great deal of bitterness at the way the whole of her immediate family had suffered. They felt that they had been cut of from their wider family and from friends and the community.

Let's put it this way, there were relations we have not
seen since we found out about Trevor ... [and] we have
only been invited to tea with Trevor once to my
brother-in-law. He thinks we should put Trevor away.

One justification for community care of mentally handicapped children, even if looking after them at home does lay a heavy burden on their mothers, is that they are thereby enabled to mix normally with other children and become assimilated into the normal life of the community. This was indeed a frequent outcome in our new city study, and where it

53

occurs it forms an important and highly desirable part of the child's
life. As with other children, not all make friends easily. In half of
the families in our sample the children were described as 'not
involved' with local children, or not interested in mixing with them,
or in two cass as positively rejected by them, or else as having few
opportunitis to mix. (The 'mild' cases, surprisingly, seemed to be a
trifle over-represented in this group.) In the other cases, however,
neighbours and neighbouring children did play a very important part in
the handicapped child's life. Involvement tends to be most intense, as
one might expect, in small village communities:

> He chucks his wheelchair around the street and everyone
> knows him, he goes in next door and has an hour in there
> and a cup of tea and biscuits, and then he goes off down
> the road, the old people love him
> ...
>
> The wheel came off his wheelchair the other day, and
> a little tot ... said 'Come quick, Edward's wheel has
> broken off his chair!' Well, I flew up ... and there were
> these five little tots, non of them were more than six (and
> he is a weight) and they had got it like this, and holding
> it so that he wouldn't go down. And their little faces!
> They really take care of him.

Urban life is also not incompatible with local involvement:

> At the moment she's in love with the boy next door. He's
> sixteen and he's a nice lad, he takes an interest in her.

Even a blind and immobile child can benefit from local involvement:

> [Her sisters'] friends come in and out. I think most of
> their friends are better with her than the grown-ups.
> Irene's ... got a friend ... orange hair one side and
> bright green the other ... If you saw her in the street
> you'd think, 'What a terrible child!' She'll come in here
> and she'll pick her up and she laughs and giggles and she's
> absolutely marvellous. But I find that all the teenagers
> and even younger ... are very, very good. It's as they get
> to our age ...

It is of course true, however, that the converse of assimilation will
also occur, and the often adverse reactions which families experience
from relatives and from the general public are one key definer of the

54

world in which the mentally handicapped child lives. Reactions range from neutral or even highly supportive (the latter particularly from the grandmothers of the children) to expressions of hostility, curiosity and distaste. One important point to note is that the parents of the mentally handicapped are of course themselves born members of the culture which despises their children, and they themslves carry these attitudes into their present situation. They may share them, or more likely fight them, or try to side-step them by aggressively declaring that their child is 'normal', but they cannot escape them; how they see their own situation is shaped, positively or negatively, by cultural norms. Indeed, to bring the argument round full circle, the reactions which they perceive others as making may be supplied at least in part and on occasion by their own expectations. The point is well illustrated in an interview with one mother in the south London sample:

> When I talk to people and I say, 'Mark is mentally handicapped', and as soon as they know he is coming up to sixteen, you see, you know what I mean? I don't want to put it into words, but you see it before they even say it ... It is an unspoken look. I suppose maybe I would be guilty in the same way, but there is that fear of danger to 'my daughter'.

However, even here the fact that the parents share, at some level, the same stigmatising stereotype as they purport to recognise in others may be responsible at least in part for creating the problem - the parents may be over-sensitive, or may even project into the situation their own unacknowledged fears and feelings of distaste (see also Bayley, 1973, p 240).

Thus having a mentally handicapped child and caring for him or her at home presents the child's parents with two major tasks which are not faced in the same way by parents of 'normal' children. They have to come to terms with the fact of the child's handicap and its implications for the way in which the family is able to conduct its normal life in interaction with others. At the same time they have to deal with the way our society labels and stigmatises mental handicap - including the way that the historically determined stereotype of mental handicap spills over as a courtesy stigma for the whole family - and this means renegotiating the nature of the family's identity and building a style of life compatible with the renegotiated identity. This task is made none the easier by the fact that the parents are themselves members of the culture which stigmatises them and their children, may project their own feelings of spoilt identity onto the world at large and share to some extent the very attitudes which they are forced to combat.

The mother's life

The work of community care, depite genuine assistance received in some cases from the family, the community and the state, tends to fall overwhelmingly on the mother. Similarly, despite the effects of handicap on the whole nuclear family which have been documented above, it is the mother's life and life-opportunities which are most disrupted by having a mentally handicapped child. The extent of the burden will of course vary from family to family; very different lives and experiences are included under the one arbitrary label of mental handicap. When the children are very young they may not present a burden of care any greater than the norm, unless there are coexistent physical problems: 'children are wonderful anyway', and mongol babies and some of the mildly retarded are particularly quiet, sweet and undemanding as infants. The 'parenting style' adopted may not be very different from that considered appropriate for the other children in the family (which demonstrates how little the discoveries of educators and therapists percolate through to the family level – see Carr, 1974, p 827). The degree of extra work may not be apparent to the mother herself because it has become 'just part of the routine'. In her survey of Scottish families Hunter (1980) asked the question 'How does having a handicapped child affect your family?' and received from one mother the answer 'It's not until somebody asks you about it that you realise what you have to do'. We had a similar experience with our own research: an interim paper was discussed at a parents' meeting and the response to the section on the work of motherhood was that they hadn't realisd until they saw it written own just how hard they did work. Nonetheless this labour and the need for it does exist, and the work falls predominantly on the child's mother.

Mothers of the mentally handicapped share with other mothers the substantial amount of work that bringing up any kind of child entails.

The mentally handicapped child requires very much more labour over a lifetime, however. The work itself will generally be more intense. For example, all children are incontinent when they are young, but mentally handicapped children are incontinent for longer. Carr (1974) foud that only 38 per cent of a sample of mongols were 'clean and dry' by day by the age of four, and only 18 per cent by night, compared with 88 per cent and 71 per cent respectively of an age-matched control sample. In a survey of Family Fund applicants (Bradshaw, 1978) almost three quarters of the 242 children over the age of four were still incontinent. Even 'mild' cases may not be trained until they are four or five, and the most severely handicapped will be incontinent well into their teens, or for ever. This means not only more years of cleaning up and extra washing, but much more to clean up - as the child grows older - and a heavier child to manoeuvre on and off the pot. Disturbance at night may also be a normal feature of life for these families for many years beyond the normal, and there may be no ready escape from it.

Worries about supervision form a second major load on mothers. Bradshaw (1980) found that nearly half of the parents who applied to the Family Fund for assistance considered that their children were at risk of harming themselves or others if left along for any period of time, and only 27 per cent felt the child could be left to play alone. We found the same kind of emphasis among the mothers to whom we spoke. The consequencs are time diverted from housework and from the other children, and a consequent extension of the 'houseworking day', sometimes late into the evening. If the mother needs to go out, even just for shopping, the more intensive child care which mentally handicapped children often require may make it difficult to find baby-sitters or child-minders or to persuade relative to share the care. (Even if it were not in fact more difficult, the parents may think that it would be, and that in itself is jsut as restricting.) Even when the children are at school the mother may need to remain 'on call', and timings have to be very precise, with very little leeway in the schedule - 'I mean, you can't really leave a handicapped child really on its own'. The child must be met from the school bus - in some cases the driver will not leave the child if there is no one there waiting. School times come to dominate the lives of such mothers even more tyranically than is normally the case:

57

> My life has been run by the school bus for fifteen years
> now. You can't go out; you must be here. From the day
> these children are born your life is planned; you've got to
> put it around that child.

In the holidays the child cannot be left even for half a day unsupervised, so school holidays are very likely to mean dropping all other activities to go back 'on guard'. Moreover, as the quotation above indicates, the process is protracted far beyond the norm. Many mothers would not leave their five year old child to come home from school to an empty house. Few, however, would still need to be there to receive a fifteen year old, with the prospect of still needing to be there when the 'child' is twenty-five.

An important part of 'community care', as envisaged by its proponents, is the notion that 'the community' will support and sustain the family in its difficulties. Half of our new city sample did indeed receive considerable help from their neighbours, ranging from transport to hospital when needed or occasional baby-sitting to more crucial interventions. Two of the mothers were able to continue work when the children were still small because neighbours took care of them. Two more had neighbours on whom they could and did call in emergencies – for example, to meet the other children from school when the handicapped child had to be taken to hospital. One mother, indeed, was able to recruit a whole street of neighbours to apply an American training programme which calls for constant stimulation of the handicapped child. Eight families, however, did not know their neighbours or received little or no help from them. The kin-group, whether or not living in the immediate neighbourhood, was another important source of help or resources for some. Mothers, mothers-in-law, cousins and siblings provided money, transport for holidays, a warm place to take the baby from a cold flat, even the occasional 'weekend off'. Half of our sample, however, did not mention any degree of help from kin. In all, six of the sixteen received help from neither the people living round them nor from their wider family, and in another five cases the help they received was comparatively trivial.

Even the help which is received from the nuclear family is not enough to change mothers' burdens appreciably. Eight mothers in our study mentioned minor help delivered by the siblings of the handicapped child – domestic work, or minor help with child-care, or in one case babysitting. One mother, a widow, received very substantial help from her eldest son. Among the fathers, five are described as helping with child-care – significant help in four cases. The contribution of six of them was not mentioned in either interview, which suggests they do as much or as little as most husbands. Five are described as doing little or nothing:

> Derek's not the sort of dad that does a lot, not knocking Derek, but I think he's an ideal man not to have kids ...

> Harry has never been like a dad should be ...

> He was very possessive, very possessive, but he never did anything to help me with him. I mean, he didn't walk till he was four. And never did he ever think of carrying him upstairs ... well, he never done anything for him. That was a woman's job.

Thus some help is received from the surroundiong community or from the kin group or indeed from within the nuclear family, but in general it is not enough to normalise the lives of the mothers who are caring for mentally handicapped children. Help from the family or from outside may carry one through an emergency or make mother's life easier or more pleasant. Nonetheless it is mother who bears the responsibility of care; others only 'help'. (Three of our mothers, indeed, mentioned no such help at all in either interview, and in two others the nuclear family was the only resource.)

Returning to a full-time job within a year or so of the birth is 'of course' out of the question for mothers of mentally handicapped children, as it appears to be for mothers of many 'normal' children (see next section). In our sample of sixteen mothers, for instance, none was currently in full-time paid employment, though all had worked before marriage. Seven had current employment of some sort – six in part-time or evening jobs, and one as a home-worker – and nine were not in employment at all. (Of this last group, however, two were already over sixty.) This kind of pattern of substantially less involvement with paid employment than is the norm even for other married women is borne out by a number of other studies (see, for example, Bayley, 1973; Glendenning, 1983). The inability to take full-time paid employment matters a great deal, because women work not only for the money (important though that may be) but also for the social contacts that

59

'going to work' brings and the increased social status which being engaged in paid employment brings in a society which devalues the domestic role.

Many of the reasons given for going down to part-time employment or giving up an outside job altogethr in our study were such as might be given by any mother, whether or not her child was labelled as handicapped: the burden of child care, the need to be at home when the children come home from school, the difficulty of school holidays, the need to take leave when the children are ill. Some explicitly denied that the child's handicap was a factor. All but four had worked at some time since the birth of their children, in an occupation which fitted school hours: school canteen asistant was popular, as were part-time jobs in shops or offices (9 till 3.30), and some had worked evenings as a cleaner or on an assembly line. One or two had done child minding or short-term fostering, or run playgroups, and several had run 'Tupperware Parties' and the like. One or two had managed a full-time job at some stage, but only because alternative child care was available. This kind of work pattern is fairly typical of any group of mothers. As we have seen, however, the mothers of the mentally handicapped have additional problems with which to contend.

People seem to be able to cope with almost anything, and most of our mothers coped with their load from day to day, trying to make a normal life for themselves and their families. On might want to distinguish, however, between families where 'normality' predominated and those where 'coping' is a more adequate descriptive term. In the latter class would fall those who would regard themselves as trying to treat the handicapped child as normal but who are resigned to the fact that they cannot entirely succeed in doing so and that the child makes a great deal of difference to their lives. They are 'resigned' to having a handicapped child rather than accepting of it, insofar as the two can be distinguished - they shade into each other. Often the problems lie with the nature of the handicap. Some children may be prone to violent outbursts, for example, out of frustration at their inability to communicate or, more worryingly, for no detectable reason. Sometimes the problem is to do with family lifestyle, as in the case of the busy mother who has three other children and manages to hold down an evening job as well when she is not child minding or undertaking short-term foster care; the (mildly) handicapped child is just a cross

60

which the family is resigned to bearing – loved and cared for, but a nuisance nonetheless. Sometimes a life which might have been comparatively easy is made difficult by the compounding pressure of other circumstances, as with Mrs Jones, a lady living on one of the rougher council estates, who appears from her own account and that of her husband to be suffering systematic persecution from a neighbouring family. In this 'coping' class we should also place 'Mrs Inglish', who is coping with life in general only with a great deal of social service support. Herself educated in a special school, and having spent a period in a psychiatric hospital, she has seldom held down a job for long; she is divorced, and the social services have assumed the parental responsibility for her children. Nonetheless, she is one who is managing to cope with the day to day care of the child.

One should remember that classifying a mentally handicapped child as 'the' problem of a family is a social construction which may not be shared by the family itself. For all the mothers we talked to the mentally handicapped child was indeed a problem, but for some there was another child about whom they worried more. Mrs Jones, for example, appeared more worried about her eldest child, who had a spell of truanting from school in response to the bullying from neighbouring children which followed on his evident grief at his grandmother's death. Another mother had a child suffering from cystic fibosis who required daily medical or nursing attention. Another had a child who had been 'teacher's pet' at a small village school and was not reacting at all well to his transfer to a larger secondary school in the new city. Mrs Inglish was far more worried by her elder son Keith than by the mentally handicapped child; Keith is a boarder at a school for maladjusted children, and he tends to beat her up and smash the furniture when he comes home on holiday.

In four of our families 'adaptation' rather than just 'coping' might be said to have taken place: the child appears to play the same role in the family as a 'normal' chld would do, and family life seems to proceed 'as normal'. (The distinction between this group and those who just cope is not a hard and fast one, however, and may be an artefact of what happened to 'come out' at particular interviews.) One middle class lady who lived in one of the neighbouring villages, for example, used to work in an office until her child was born, went back to similar work when the child was three, and now (in her forties) does

61

some work as a cook in the local school. She spends a great deal of time with her child and has to some extent 'built her life around her', but one has the impression that this would have been her pattern of life if the child had not been handicapped; she seems happy and settled. Another continued with part-time office work all the time she lived near relatives who could babysit, helped her husband for two years when he was running his own business, and is currently looking round for a part-time job which would involve her with children. She seems very close to and involved with both her children equally and to enjoy the life she has with them. Another lady with three children (one mildly retarded, and one with cystic fibrosis) presented herself in interview very much as a classic 'working class mum'. She switched from full- to part-time factory work when she married, went over to working in the evenings when her first child was born, and switched again to cooking in a canteen when the others were born in order to be more available when they came out of school. The mentally handicapped child appears to have presented few problems once he was out of nappies and to be treated very much like her eldest, normal child. The fourth lady found she had to give up work to look after her children – apart from the odd cleaning job and running the occasional 'Tupperware Party' – because her husband's long and irregular hours of work as a self-employed carpet fitter meant that he could not take regular responsibility for them. At the end of her interview, however, she surprised herself by saying:

> I think family life is important, and I mean, we are a
> normal family. My cousin said that one. I thought it was
> a queer thing to say. She said, 'I like it because you
> don't treat Edith anything but normal', and I said, 'Well,
> how the hell am I supposed to treat her?' But I thought
> about it afterwards and I suppose I could see what she
> meant, she wasn't being funny. We don't go out of our way
> because I've got a backward child, we don't not do
> anything, we do everything that, in fact, a normal family
> does.

These were all cases of a normal, unremarkable adaptation to family life. In six of our sixteen interviews, however, it is possible to detect a more exaggerated and systematic 'style' of adaptation. One mother, for instance, describes herself as very much enjoying married

62

life and seeing children as an important and integral part of it.
After school she worked in a shop, then took evening clases and became
a clerk, but she gave up work when she 'fell for' her first child - a
pre-marital but planned pregnancy. She has done odd jobs since -
cleaning in the evenings, and lunch-time jobs - but she feels she could
not take a settled job because of the handicapped child. However, she
says she would not take a full-time job even if he were not there,
because her other (older) child needs her at home. Another lady, Mrs
Allinson, has not held a job since her handicapped daughter was born,
and she very much enjoys not doing so; despite the amount of effort she
puts into her life, she regards herself as something of a 'lady of
leisure'. A third lady aspired to the same style. Talking of her
early aspirations, she lists the chief one as 'just wanting to get
married and have a family', and she says she looked forward to not
working as a relief. Hoever, she has found caring for her two children
very hard work; only now that they both go out to school is she
beginning to enjoy the leisure to which she had looked forward. The
fourth started her working life in a factory, but she did not enjoy it
and was very glad to quit after she was married, when she 'fell for'
her first child. She is beginning to think of taking some kind of
part-time job, but that would be some considerable time in the future,
as her oldest is only six.

These people might be seen, perhaps, as 'having marriage as a
career' rather than just as being married. Another 'career' which one
might detect in two of the interviews is that of child-minding. One
lady, for example, had a family of five children spread over nine years
and was then told she was very unlikely to be able to have any more.
Eight years later, when she had supposed she was menopausal, she
conceived 'by accident' and bore a severely brain damaged child. (She
promptly had her seventh child, to provide him with company.) He is
now sixteen, with an assessed mental age of about five but a 'social
age' (we met him) which presents as very similar to his chronological
age. She is now sixty, and he is very much the companion of her old
age, while she is probably his closest friend and companion.

    He has been a marvellous child, he hs given me lots and
    lots of pleasure ... He'll stay. He won't be any
    different to what he is now ... By the time I do go ...

we're all long livers in my family ... he'll have had a
good life, as good as anyone could give him.

The second lady in this category says of herself that

I've looked after young children all my life. I was always
baby-minded, taking them out for walks. Very baby-minded
person, when I was very young ... that was my one aim in
life, to have loads and loads of children ... I like
children, you know, I like to be surrounded by children.

Of the 'respite' weekends that have been arranged for her, when Gerry
goes into a hospital, she says

It has taken me an awful long time to part with her even
for odd weeks ... I didn't trust them, anyway, with her,
to think that they could just automatically cope with her.
So it's continuously on the 'phone every day, 'phoning up.
It took me about - four she was the first time I let her go
in - until eleven before I really knew who I was talking
to.

That the reluctance to let her go was not just related to the quality
of her care is emphasised later in the interview:

[Husband] You see, the first idea of relief care, whether
it sounds harsh or not, was to get Lorna used to not having
her around ... The idea in the beginning was to take her
for longer and longer periods, so that she wouldn't be
dependent on Gerry. You know, she wouldn't run her life.

[Wife] I think I should be lost without her: because my
whole life does centre around her.

This case also provides a good illustration of how one's 'world
picture' may change over time and how 'motivation' may sometimes be
shaped teleologically to validate an outcome which is judged
inevitable. At the time of our first interview she very definitely
appeared to see herself as a child-centred person whos future employmet
would be in child-care or in the care of the elderly - at least in part
as a substitute for the daughter around whom her life had been centred
until now. She confirmed in the second interview, a year later, that
this had indeed been her picture of herself at the time and that she
would indeed still feel lost and without purpose when Gerry has to go -
that she might even break down at that point. However, since the first
interview she had taken and passed a typing course and had every hope

64

that she might obtain an office job at some time in the future if jobs of any kind were to be had. She now regards her earlier picture of her future as at least in part a rationalisation of the inevitable.

In summary, the mother of the mentally handicapped child carries the same burden as any other mother – the burden of child care. This may be willingly accepted or even sought out and planned for, but it is nonetheless a life-consuming role which leaves little time or space for individuality. In that sense these mothers' lives are 'normal' for women, statistically and in terms of role-expectation, but as remote from the lives of men as are most married women's lives. Over and above the 'normal' constraints of other mothers, however, these women live a life more closely packed with problems, and the problems go on for a substantially longer period. This is the non-financial cost of community care.

Comparison with the 'normal'

Shortly after the second interviews with mothers of mentally handicapped children, one of us conducted a series of interviews with a 'sample' of mothers whose children had not been labelled as mentally handicapped, roughly matched for size of family and area of residence (which correlates well, in the new city, both with social class and with availability of 'social resources'). The sample is of course too small and haphazard to be representative of mothers in general – and a similar charge might be levelled at the sample of mothers of the mentally handicapped – but the two samples match closely enough for some tentative comparisons to be drawn. One can after all say little about what is distinctive in the experience of mothering mentally handicapped children except by comparison with the generally experience of mothering.

Compared with our 'mental handicap' sample, very few of these mothers commented on the amount of work which having children around the house entails. Ten had no particular comment to make at all, except (in four cases) to say that they did not enjoy housework. Five, on the other hand, expressed positive pleasure in domestic work. For example:

I'm just that kind of person, I like to be tidy ... I like to do everything ... so that when I come home all I have to

do really is tidy up in general down here, and give them a
good cooked meal.
(Mrs Blacker)

People I know sit around and say 'I get bored', but I
don't honestly get time. If I'm not gardening I'm
decorating and if I'm not decorating I'm making – I do all
my own dressmaking. If I'm not dressmaking I'm
embroidering or knitting. Oh yes, I make the wine, I do
the lot.
(Mrs Greene)

Washing their clothes, cooking for them, that's not
hard work because it's a natural thing.
(Mrs Royal)

Another lady described how she managed to render housework interesting
by treating it as a nine-to-five job on the one hand and never letting
it settle into an exact routine on the other. Only four people
commented on the strains of the housewife's work, and their comments
were to do mostly with how little sleep one seems to have during the
first few years of a child's life.

One could well form the impression, in contradistinction to the
mothers of mentally handicapped children, that these mothers did not
regard the daily and yearly grind of motherhood as particularly hard
work. This may to an extent be true: while mothering ordinary children
is undoubtedly hard work, as anyone will testify who has children in
the house, it is equally undoubtedly not as much work as mothering most
mentally handicapped children. It differs in two other ways as well:
(1) the children of these mothers were often of similar chronological
ages to the children who appeared in the last section, but for this
reason they were mostly more advanced in terms of development – the
messier and heavier work lay in the past – and (2) the work entailed by
a normal child has a forseeable termination, which often means that it
seems less onerous. It may be also that mothers under-rate the work of
being a housewife precisely because it is 'normal', taken for granted
by everybody concerned, while the mothering of a mentally handicapped
child leads one to think about the work involved. Two other factors
should also be considered, however. First, our sample under-represents
women in full-time paid employment, which could well make a difference
– though the two women in our sample who were in full time employment

66

were not among the ones who commented on the pains of housework. The second factor is that the interviewer was male; it is possible that different things might have been said to a female interviewer.

As regards help with the work, we formed the impression from the interviews that the mothers of the unlabelled children received much the same help and support from kin, but more from neighbours, than did the mothers of the mentally handicapped children – that they were more closely integrated into the local community. Of the nineteen that we interviewed, twelve can be described as receiving (or having received in the past, when the children were younger) a fair amount of help from kin or neighbours or both, and another two as having received occasional or emergency help. The parents and/or parents-in-law of six of the families lived in the neighbourhood, and four of them had received a good deal of help with child rearing or child care. One has a sister who takes the children overnight, and another a mother who advises and provides practical help (and neices who babysit whenever required). Mrs Scarlett stayed with her mother for a few days after her second child was born, to give her time to recuperate while not interfering with her husband's ability to work. Another of these ladies would say that her family were not on the whole a great source of help, but her mother has been over once or twice a week during the current pregnancy, to do housework and ironing and anything else that she judged too much of a strain for a pregnant woman. Two others did not now see much of their parents, but they were a great source of help before they moved from London to the new city. For example, when Mrs Forrest's first child was a baby her husband's parents lived just round the corner, and her own were only seven miles away, so babysitting was never a problem and they were able to go out – in the evening or during the day – whenever they wanted to do so. (With her later children she has been more restricted in that respect, but her parents come up for the weekend not infrequently, and Mrs Forrest and her husband generally take advantage of the situation.) Six informants out of the nineteen rarely saw their parents or received little help from them, and seven had little or nothing to say about kin, but for six the 'extended family' was an important resource. This is much the same picture as emerged from the analyses in the last section – round about a third receiving significant help from the extended family.

A different picture emerges when we look at involvement with neighbours and the local community. Eight of the mothers of mentally handicapped children said they received little or no help from their neighbours, but only five of the mothers of unlabelled children were in this position. Seven of the nineteen had a great deal of help from their neighbours - invaluable help in some cases, making the desired lifestyle possible rather than impracticable.

> The neighbours are super ... I've always had a babysitter ... If I want to go to bed at ten in the morning and I've worked [on the night shift] the night before, my daughter gets her little shopping bag and go off down [to a neighbour] ... and goes with them to school ... You just couldn't do these things without neighbours.
>
> (Mrs Whiting)

Four others mentioned occasional help, and two help in emergencies. Overall only five of the mothers of 'unlabelled' children had little or no help from either kin or neighbours, and twelve had a great deal of help from one or the other or both. In comparison, eleven of the mothers of mentally handicapped children received either no help at all or only trivial assistance.

As regards help from within the nuclear family, six of our informants' husbands are described realistically (we checked by asking what they actually did about the house) as taking a share or doing a great deal. For example:

> Whoever comes in first starts the dinner. You do the cooking [to her husband] and some of the cleaning. I think you have to, because we both go out now, doing different things.
>
> (Mrs Olivier)

> My husband does housework, he's tidier than I am, actually. The other night I was out ... I didn't get home till ten, and there he was ironing. He always bathes the kids ... He can cook dinner. I went to France on a day trip ... and he had the children all day, and his Dad, he was out of hospital for the weekend ... he cooked them a dinner and took them to the park.
>
> (Mrs Blacker)

68

I suppose it's because I hate [housework] that they
all do their bit, even the five year old does a bit around
the house ... The oldest boy cooks the dinner if ever
we're not there ... [My husband] probably does more than I
do, to be honest. I think he always has probably done more
... because we've both always worked ... If it came to say
who is really boss in the kitchen, he would be ... Two
weeks out of three he does the shopping ... He probably
taught me most of what I know about cooking anyway ...
He'll do anything and everything around the house.
(Mrs Whiting)

I don't very often ask him to now, but when I had the
children ... he did ironing and different things ... If
I'm not well ... he'll just come in and take over. When we
were first married and both working, he'd come in and maybe
wash up while I hoovered and things like that.
(Mrs Forrest)

Another lady described how her husband will take over getting the
supper and send her up to have a bath, when he gets in from work, if he
thinks she looks under the weather, and how he has done her evening
cleaning job once or twice when she has been ill. Seven others
describe their husbands as doing a bit about the house - childcare (3)
or housework (1) or both (3) - but only in the sense of 'helping'. Six
others described their husbands as offering little or no daily help.
Adding these in, this still leaves three families where the wife
receives virtually no help in keeping up the house and looking after
the children, from nuclear family or kin or neighbours. The same
number were without help in the families with mentally handicapped
children.

Overall, then, the mothers of the unlabelled children and the
mothers · of the mentally handicapped children had much the same
resources to draw on in their 'home work', with the exception that the
mothers of unlabelled children seemed to receive more help from the
surrounding community. One should not over-rate the amount or quality
of the help, however, in the majority of cases. While a few of our
informants praised their husbands for the amount of work they did
around the house and/or with the children, in only two cases were they
prepared to say that the husband did as much (or more) as they did

themselves, or that they could relinquish responsibility for the work. This is the general finding of research into husbands' involvement in the work of the home. Men may on occasion be substantially involved in childcare – and perhaps increasingly so – but seldom in the remaining work of the house (though if mothers are asked not which tasks the husband undertakes but how often he undertakes them or how many hours he spends on them, it turns out that nerly fifty per cent of married men with children can best be described as only minimally involved in childcare – see Boulton, 1983). As regards housework, Edgell's 1980 study suggests that virtually no husbands take an equal share, and nearly half do virtually none. The families whom we have interviewed do not seem to be as extreme – there were a few cases of genuine help, within the limitation of work constraints – but we also formed the impression that most women nonetheless receive precious little help in the day-to-day running of the house, and certainly that the running of the house remains the woman's responsibility in the vast majority of cases.

In this context, Backett (1982) has pointed out in relation to her study of couples in an Edinburgh suburb that:

> In order for couples to sustain belief in [high] levels of father involvement they did not see it as necessary for him to participate fully or constantly. Rather it is a matter of each couple negotiating the kind of practical proof which they found to be subjectively satisfactory. This was done by the father's participating sufficiently regularly in those particular spheres which spouses had identified as being relevant to their own family situation. (p.221)

She also points out that the situation for men is fundamentally different from the situation for women, where the man goes out to work and the wife stays at home. When the husband is at home, even if he were literally to take an equal share of available 'home work', it is a share; his wife is there to carry the other half. Thus a man may 'do' childcare, or housework, and be fully committed to it. Never or seldom, however, is he faced with the daily problem that his wife faces when he is not at home – that both houswork and childcare have to be coped with at one and the same time.

70

In the sample of sixteen mothers of mentally handicapped children, described in the last section, none was in full-time paid employment at the time of the interview. Six were in part-time or evening jobs, one was a home worker, and nine were not working at all. Of our sample of nineteen mothers whose children were not labelled as mentally handicapped, two were in full time employment (a proportion which undoubtedly underrates the proportion in the population – those we approached who were in full-time employment tended to decline the interview), six were in a substantial part-time job, two did some part-time paid work and some voluntary work, one was substantially involved in voluntary work (as a WI county organiser), and three others did a small amount of part-time work or home work and helped out at their children's schools. Only five were in no form of employment, and one of those was in a late stage of pregnancy. The two groups differ substantially on this variable, therefore: the mothers or mentally handicapped children were markedly less able to take outside employment.

However, we should note that the presence of children in the home still made a substantial difference to the pattern of employment. Of those who worked full-time, one was on the night shift (as a nurse) so that there was always someone in the house to look after the children. Of the eight who were in part-time employment, six had jobs deliberately chosen to leave them free to be home when the children came home from school (morning work in a garage office, day-time shifts as a nurse, or the jobs in canteens or as school welfare officers which are so popular with mothers). There were no cases of men similarly curtailing their work patterns in the interests of the children. The responsibility for the children's welfare still falls disproportionately on the mothers, therefore, even if they are freer to take paid employment in the interests of their childcare job.

Other factors which were evident in the 'mental handicap' interviews were far less salient in the other ones. Mothers of mentally handicapped children talked a great deal about the difficulties of being tied to the timetable of the child, which was a minority response among the other mothers interviewed; the unlabelled children remained children in that sense for a much shorter period before they could be trusted to look after themselves to some limited extent. The initial adaptation to the child was of course a major theme in the interviews with mothers of mentally handicapped children and not in the others, though there were a few comments about the difficulty of adapting to the lack of freedom (and of sleep!) which young children entail. Most noticeable was the relative absence in the interviews with mothers of unlabelled children of comments about the longer-term adaptations which the family had undergone and of the family's plans for the future. It seemed taken for granted in the majority of cases that having children was a temporary phase, though of long duration, yet on the other hand there was relatively little conscious planning for the future. One had the impression more of a state of faith that the future would take care of itself in a relatively unproblematic way, 'as it does for everybody else'.

The family's future

'In the normal course of things' children grow from babies to toddlers, go to school and become increasingly independent in their lives there, leave school, find a job (or, increasingly, fail to do so) and eventually cease to be the responsibility of their parents. As we have seen, mentally handicapped children generally go through the early stages of this life-course more slowly than others and thereby create substantial burdens which generally fall on their mothers. In their adolescence, however, they may constitute a substantial problem for both parents, because for some of them there is every likelihood that they will never leave home at all unless their parents make specific arrangements to send them aeay. As Dickerson and Brown (1978) have pointed out, the parents

> ... have one child who is not going to release them from responsibility. It gets to be a very big worry. Who is going to support this child? Who will pay the bills? Provide him a good home? Supervise his leisure time ...? Keep him out of trouble ...? The parents find that they need to make long-term arrangements for the disabled child in the event of their deaths.

In the shorter term, the children leave school at some time in their teens and may therefore no longer be 'off their parents' hands' during the day.

One of the problems is that handicapped children grow less wonderful as they grow older. What was acceptable appearance and behaviour in someone who looks five or ten years old may no longer be acceptable in someone who looks twenty or thirty. Several of the mothers in the South London sample commented on this problem, and one had even had her daughter institutionalised to avoid the expected problems:

> This is one reason why something would have to be done. She went into the hospital ... when she was 21. Caroline was 3 and Michael was 19, coming up to 20. I have seen so many families where the brothers have girlfriends and this causes unpleasantness, and ... I said we have got to do something before Michael starts going serious with girlfriends, before Caroline goes to school and brings friends home. We don't want to make any unpleasantness.

At the same time, the mentally handicapped child may paradoxically become relatively younger – more of a burden to the family – in proportion as he or she becomes older physically. Even if no more of a burden, the 'child' remains the same burden for year after year in a 'frozen' family which has lost the space to change and in which the parents themselves are becoming older and less able to cope.

While the family's development is frozen, however, social provision is not: the provision for a family with a handicapped child tends if anything to decline as the 'child' grows past school age. The real 'community care' for mentally handicapped children who grow into mentally handicapped adults is that they follow the 'normal' pattern and leave home – for a hostel and sheltered work, for a farm community or a group home, or for a hospital. For most families the time when children leave home is in any case a 'crisis-point', but for the families of the mentally handicapped it is likely in addition to involve great feelings of guilt, because the child is generally not leaving home 'naturally' but being 'pushed out'. In the sixteen families we interviewed in the new city only one mother saw her retarded child as likely to leave home and live a normal life; this was a mildly handicapped child of fourteen who was already showing every sign of being able to cope adequately and whose retarded uncles were coping in the outside world. Six others thought their child would always stay at home with them, but half of these were also considering the possibility of placement in a hostel or a sheltered community when they became unable to cope. Two (whose childen were aged respectively eight and five) had not considered the topic. The other seven were already beginning negotiation for a hostel place or a place in a resdential school or community. Thus well over half of our sample had to deal in their minds with the possibility or the likelihood of handing care over to others, and of these seven were expecting or fearing that the care would have to be in some sort of institution. The very childishness which make the child a burden at home and necessitates the arrangements for continuity of care, paradoxically, increase the stress and the guilt of relocation:

When you think what her mental age is, say four or five, by the time she's nineteen it won't be much more than that.

You wouldn't stick a five year old in a hostel, would you?

The choice of a proper institution or facility and the battle to be accepted there – as funds, and therefore places, are limited – can be a problem before which all earlier problems seem trivial and manageable.

Conclusions

To recapitulate, then, we have looked in this paper at the real costs of bearing and bringing up a mentally handicapped child in the community. Some of it – the day to day grind of 'child work' – falls largely on the child's mother, though her involvement in it has consequencs for the rest of the family. The rearing of a mentally handicapped baby does not differ in kind from the rearing of any other baby – itself a substantial social burden – but it differs in its density and its duration. The care of a retarded child may require constant vigilance, and the lateness of normal 'stages of development' doubles or trebles the burden of an 'ordinary' problem such as incontinence. The burden goes on, moreover, potentially for ever, unless the decision is made to send the child away – to the point where aging parents can no longer cope or provision must be made for what happens after their death or in the case of their eventual incapacity. (The potential exceptions – at least three out of our sample of sixteen – are those whose children are not expected to live beyond their twenties; some of the mental handicaps have coexistent physical problems of great severity.) Specific to mental handicap, however, are

74

the other major range of problems which families encounter: the reactions which the notion of mental handicap engenders in our culture, among strangers and also within the family and kin group. Not least of this range of problems is that the parents of the retarded are themselves a part of the culture which stereotypes retardation and have to cope with their own reactions and their expectations of how others will react as well as with the real situation.

POSTSCRIPT

In the first of these two papers we argued that an understanding of how mental handicap is currently perceived and 'treated' can only be reached by looking at the way perceptions and treatment have been shaped by historical forces. In the second paper we have illustrated how mothers of mentally handicapped children are expected to take on an additional burden in the Britain of the 1980s, as care in the community has been increasingly advocated and adopted as the main method of handling mentally handicapped people. (Elsewhere – see Abbott, 1982; Abbott and Sapsford, 1983 – we have explored social and economic factors underlying the change of policy towards 'community care', which has become in practice merely 'care in the community'.) The latter paper shows the entire willingness with which most of the mothers take on the additional burdens, accept that it is right that they should do so, and are prepared to adapt their lives and expectations to their circumstances. While some mothers point to the adverse consequences that this has had for other family members few seem to see themselves as disadvantaged.

For this failure of vision one might in turn advance a historical explanation. Attitudes of mothers follow, in a sense, from the way that historically the private sphere of home, domestic work and childcare has become separated from world of 'work' and politics, and from the consequent ideology of motherhood which developed as Britain developed its industrial capitalism in the nineteenth century. Furthermore, we would contend that official policies of community care reflect and reinforce that ideology: the nuclear family of husband as 'provider' and wife as 'home maker' is seen not just as how people choose to live, but also as how they ought to live. Welfare reforms in the twentieth century have accepted this situation as the norm, and thereby reinforced it. To a large extent state welfare provision depends on the fact that women (apparently willingly) take on responsibility for the care of dependent groups – whether these be, eg, children under five, the elderly or the mentally handicapped – and that they will do so without payment. In other words, we can only understand fully why mothers are prepared to take on this burden of care when we examine the ideology which underlies their 'choice'. This ideology determines and justifies the form that the subordination of women takes in capitalist society. State legislation and welfare

76

provision sustains and reinforces the ideology as well as being shaped by it. How we treat mental handicap, as a society and as individuals, illustrates the general nature of our social living and our constructions of self: individuals may respond individually to their circumstances, and these circumstances may in fact vary widely within a group classed arbitrarily together for purpose of analysis, but what they hold in common is a set of socioeconomic structures and a history embodied in ideology and institutions which together shape and constrain both state action and individual understanding.

REFERENCES

ABBOTT PA (1982), Towards a Social Theory of Mental Handicap, PhD thesis, CNAA/Thames Polytechnic.

ABBOTT PA and SAPSFORD RJ (1983), Mental Handicap and Motherhood: An Interim Report, The Open University, Social Science Working Papers.

ABBOTT PA and SAPSFORD RJ (1986), 'Diverse reports: caring for mentally handicapped children in the community', Nursing Times, 5 March, 47–49.

AUDEN G (1909), Report of the Medical Superintendent for Birmingham, 1909.

AUDEN G (1912), Report of the Medical Superintendent for Birmingham, 1912.

BACKETIT KC (1982), Mothers and Fathers: A Study of the Development and Negotiation of Parental Behaviour, Macmillan.

BARR MW (1904), Mental Defectives: Their History and Treatment and Training, Blackston.

BARTON R (1959), Institutional Neurosis, Wright.

BAYLEY M (1973), Mental Handicap and Community Care, Routledge and Kegan Paul.

BEACH F (1895), The Treatment and Education of Mentally Feeble Children, Churchill.

BERNSTEIN C (1920), 'Colony and extra-institutional care for the feebleminded', Mental Hygiene 4, 1–29.

BEVERIDGE Lord (1906), 'The problem of the unemployed', Sociology Papers 3.

BIRENBAUM A (1970), 'On managing a courtesy stigma', Journal of Health, 196–206.

BLUMER H (1971), 'Social problems as collective behaviour', Social Problems, 18, 298–306.

BOARD OF CONTROL (1927), Lunacy and Mental Deficiency: Thirteenth Report of the Board of Control.

BOULTON MG (1983), On Being a Mother: A Study of Women with Pre-School Children, Tavistock.

BOWLBY J (1954), Maternal Deprivation, Penguin.

BOWLES S and GINTIS A (1976), Schooling in Capitalist America, Routledge and Kegan Paul.

BRADSHAW J (1978), Incontinence: A Burden for Families, London, Disabled Living Foundation.

BRADSHAW J (1980), The Family Fund: An Initiative in Social Policy, Routledge and Kegan Paul.

BUCKLE J (1984), Mental Handicap Costs More, Disablement Income Group Charitable Trust.

BURT CL (1913), 'The inheritance of mental characteristics', Eugenics Review 4.

CARR J (1975), Young Children with Downs Syndrome: Their Development, Upbringing and Effects on Their Families, Butterworth.

CHARITIES ORGANISATION SOCIETY (1877), Report of a Sub-Committee on the Education and Care of Idiots, Imbeciles and Harmless Lunatics, Longman, Green.

CONDILLAC B (1755), 'Traite des Sensations' in Abbe de Mably (ed) (1798), Oeuvres de Condillac.

CUMMINGS ST (1976), 'The impact of the child's deficiency on the father: a study of fathers of mentally retarded and chronically ill children', American Journal of Orthopsychiatry 46, 246-55.

DAVENPORT CB (1911), Heredity in Relation to Eugenics, Holt.

DEFOE D (1697), An Essay Upon Projects, Cockerill.

DEPARTMENT OF HEALTH AND SOCIAL SECURITY (1971), Better Services for the Mentally Handicapped, HMSO, Cmnd 4683.

DEPARTMENT OF HEALTH AND SOCIAL SECURITY (1978), Review of the Mental Health Act 1959, HMSO.

DEPARTMENT OF HEALTH AND SOCIAL SECURITY (1979), Report of the Committee of Enquiry into Mental Handicap Nursing and Training (the Jay Report), HMSO.

DEPARTMENT OF HEALTH AND SOCIAL SECURITY (1981a), Report of a Study on Community Care, DHSS.

DEPARTMENT OF HEALTH AND SOCIAL SECURITY (1981b), Care in the Community: a Consultative Document on Moving Resources for Care in England, DHSS.

DEUTSCH (1949), The Mentally Ill in America: A History of Their Care and Treatment second edition, Doubleday, Doran.

DICKERSON M and BROWN S (1978), 'A search for a family' in S Brown and M Moersch (eds), Parents on the Team, University of Michigan Press.

DOLL E (1929), 'Community control of the feebleminded', Journal of Psycho-Asthenics 34, 161-75.

DOWN JL (1867), 'Observations on an ethnic classification of idiots', Mental Science 13, 121-8.

DOWN JL (1887), On Some Mental Afflictions of Childhood and Youth, Churchill.

DUGDALE RL (1877), The Jukes: A Study in Crime, Pauperism, Disease and Heredity, Putnam.

EDGELL S (1980), Middle-Class Couples: A Study of Segregation, Domination and Inequality in Marriage, Allen and Unwin.

ESTABROOK AH (1916), The Jukes in 1913, Carnegie Institute.

ESTABROOK AH and **MCDOUGLE I** (1926), Mongrel Virginians, Carnegie Institute.

FERNALD WE (1912), 'The burden of feeblemindedness', Journal of Psycho-Asthenics 17, 87-111.

FINCH J and GROVES D (1983), A Labour of Love: Women, Work and Caring, Routledge and Kegan Paul.

FOUCAULT M (1971), Madness and Civilisation, Tavistock.

FOUCAULT M (1976), Mental Illness and Psychology, Harper Colophon.

GALLAGHER JJ, BECKMAN P and CROSS AH (1983), 'Families of handicapped children: sources of stress and its amelioration', Exceptional Children 50, 10-19.

GALTON F (1869), Hereditary Genius, Peter Smith (1972).

GLENDINNING C (1983), Unshared Care: Parents and their Disabled Children, Routledge and Kegan Paul.

GODDARD HH (1910), 'Heredity in Feeblemindedness', American Breeders Magazine 1, 165-78.

GODDARD HH (1912), The Kallikak Family: A Study in the Heredity of Feeblemindedness, Macmillan.

GOFFMAN E (1961), Asylums, Anchor Books.

GOFFMAN E (1963), Stigma: the Management of Spoilt Identities, Penguin (1968).

GREENGROSS W (1976), Entitled to Love?, Marriage Guidance Council.

HOWE SG (1848), 'Report made to the legislature of Massachussets upon idiocy', Senate 51, February.

HUNTER ABJ (1980), The Family and their Mentally Handicapped Child, Barnardo Social Work papers no 12.

IRELAND WW (1849), The Mental Afflictions of Children: Idiocy, Imbecility and Insanity, Churchill.

ITARD J (1801), 'The wild boy of Aveyron: of the first developments of the young savage of Aveyron' in L Malson (ed) (1976), Wolf Children, New Left Books.

80

ITARD J (1807), 'Report on the progress of Victor of Aveyron' in L Malson (ed), op cit.

JOHNSON GE (1902), 'Contribution to the psychology and pedology of feebleminded children', Journal of Psycho-Asthenics, September.

JONES K (1972), A History of the Mental Health Services, Routledge and Kegan Paul.

KING RD, RAYNES NV and TIZARD J (1971), Patterns of Residential Care, Routledge and Kegan Paul.

LAPAGE CP (1920), Feeblemindedness in Children of School Age, Manchester University Press.

LOCKE J (1690), An Essay Concerning Human Understanding, Barnet.

LYLE J (1958), 'The effect of an institutional environment upon the verbal development of imbecile children I: verbal intelligence', Journal of Mental Deficiency 3, 122-8.

LYLE J (1959a) 'The effect of an institutional environment upon the verbal development of imbecile children II: speech and language', Journal of Mental Deviciency 4, 1-13.

LYLE J (1959b) 'The effect of an institutional environment upon the verbal development of imbecile children III: the Brooklands Residential Family Unit', Journal of Mental Deficiency 4, 14-22.

MOREL BA (1860), Le Non-Restraint, ou de l'Abolition des Moyens Coercifs dans le Traitment de la Folie.

NATIONAL COUNCIL FOR CIVIL LIBERTIES (1951), 50,000 Outside the Law; NCCL.

NEUGEBAUER R (1978), 'Treatment of the mentally ill in medieval and early modern England: a reappraisal', Journal of the History of the Behavioural Sciences 14, 158-69.

NORRIS D (1975), Day Care and Severe Handicap, British Association for the Retarded.

PEARSON K (1905), 'National deterioration', The Times 25 August.

POLITICAL AND ECONOMIC PLANNING (1937), Report on the British Health Service, PEP.

ROSEN G (1968), Madness in Society: Chapters in the Historical Sociology of Mental Illness, University of Chicago Press.

ROSEN G (1974), From Medical Police to Social Medicine, Neale Watson.

ROYAL COMMISSION (1909), The Problem of the Feebleminded: An Abstract of the Report of the Royal Commission on the Care and Control of the Feebleminded, PS King.

RUSSELL B (1924), Icarus, or the Future of Science, Kegan Paul.

SCHERENBERGER RC (1983), A History of Mental Retardation, Brookes.

SCULL AT (1977), Decarceration: Community Treatment and the Deviant, Prentice-Hall.

SEGUIN E (1846), Traitement Moral, Hygiene et Education des Idiots et des outres Enfants Arrieres, Baliere Tindall.

SHEARER A (1972), A Report on Public and Professional Attitudes Towards the Sexual and Emotional Attitudes of Handicapped People, Spastics Society/National Association for Mental Handicap.

SHUTTLEWORTH GE and POTTS WA (1895), Mentally Deficient Children: Their Treatment and Training, Lewis.

SMILES S (1859), Self-Help: The Art of Achievement Illustrated by Accounts of the Lives of Great Men.

SPENCER H (1851), Social Statics, Kelley (1969).

TALBOT ES (1898), Degeneracy.

TIZARD J (1964), Community Care for the Mentally Handicapped, Oxford University Press.

TREDGOLD AF and SODDY K (eds) (1970), Tredgold's Mental Retardation eleventh edition, Baliere, Tindall and Cox.

TRUSTEES OF THE STATE OF NEW YORK SCHOOL FOR IDIOTS (1852), Report of the Trustees for 1852.

US DEPARTMENT OF COMMERCE (1914), Annual Report of the Secretary of Commerce, 1914, Government Printing Office.

WALKER A (1982), Community Care: the Family, the State and Social Policy, Blackwell and Robertson.

WALKER N and McCABE S (1973), Crime and Insanity in England vol II, University of Edinburgh Press.

WEBB S (1906), 'Physical degeneracy or race suicide', The Times 11 October and 16 October.

WEEKS J (1981), Sex, Politics and Society: The Regulation of Sexuality Since 1800, London, Longman.

WILLIS T (1672), De Anima Brutorum translated (1863) by S Pardage as Two Discourses Concerning the Soul of Brutes.

WING JK and BROWN GW (1970), Institutionalism and Schizophrenia, Cambridge University Press.

WOLFENSBERGER W (1970), 'Models of Mental Retardation', New Society 15, 51-3.

WOLFENSBERGER W (1976), The Origins and Nature of our Institutional Models, Human Policy Press.

WORLD HEALTH ORGANISATION (1954), The Mentally Subnormal Child, WHO Technical Report Series no 75.